Accelerated Paces:
Travels Across Borders and Other Imaginary Boundaries

Accelerated Paces:

Travels Across Borders and Other Imaginary Boundaries

Jim Oaten

anvIL
PRESS

Anvil Press Inc.
P.O. Box 3008, Main Post Office
Vancouver, B.C. V6B 3X5 CANADA
www.anvilpress.com

First Printing.

Library and Archives Canada Cataloguing in Publication

Oaten, Jim
  Accelerated paces : travels across borders and other
imaginary boundaries / Jim Oaten.

ISBN 978-1-895636-93-2

  I. Title.

PS8629.A84A73 2008   C813'.6   C2008-904947-0

Printed and bound in Canada
Cover design: Derek von Essen
Interior design & typesetting: HeimatHouse
Author photo: Gavin Lynch

Represented in Canada by the Literary Press Group
Distributed by the University of Toronto Press

The publisher gratefully acknowledges the financial assistance of
the Canada Council for the Arts, the Book Publishing Industry
Development Program (BPIDP), and the Province of British
Columbia through the BC Arts Council and the Book
Publishing Tax Credit.

For Sheena

ACKNOWLEDGEMENTS:

Previous versions of some of these pieces have appeared in *subTerrain*, *The Vancouver Sun*, *Pacific Rim Magazine*, and *The Peak*.

Grateful thanks to the crew at Anvil Press, and to all my family and friends . . . for everything.

Table of Contents

Even as a ghost
My Spirit will want to roam
The fields of summer.

—Hokusai

Stardust

I am young, and we are driving. Where, I don't really know. At that age, such things were never my concern. Destinations lay in the adult world; I was just along for the ride.

As always, my father holds the wheel. My mother plays her role, sending out an endless stream of cheerful chatter, none of which we really need respond to. Top-40 hits from days gone by quietly slide out from the oldies station my father always seems to find, no matter how often I surreptitiously reprogram the radio.

Black and white flashes by. "Oh look, cows—aren't they lovely," says my mom to no one in particular. Frank Sinatra sings yet another song about love.

"Love is now the stardust of yesterday. The music of the years gone by...."

Beside me, my brother. He is even younger. I am belt-less in those carefree days of solid-steel cars and rust-induced obsolescence. He is strapped down, and wriggling against the booster seat like a fur seal straining out of Arctic ice. I like it when he's belted tight: it keeps him away from my toys.

"Back home, the cows were never that pretty. They were hairy, weren't they Bob?" My father hisses agreement as he hunts for a spot to overtake the crawling car in front.

A triumphant yawp from my brother. He's managed to get one of my toys after all: a Hot Wheels that unwisely skidded across the seat when my father finally eyed his chance and accelerated onto the other side of the road. It's an old one, not a favourite and I let him have it. He chews happily.

"Car," he says, smiling at me. Drool drips from the Hot Wheels' hood.

Wheatfield, wheatfield, wheatfield, truckstop. Wheatfield, wheatfield, wheatfield. Tires hum and drag the scenery by.

"*Sometimes I wonder why I spend the lonely nights dreaming of a song*," ponders Frank.

"And they were mostly brown, too. Nasty things. Remember?" asks Mom.

"Are we there yet?" I inquire.

"Cookie?" wonders my brother, lips crammed with car.

My father hisses in answer to all as we speed through the flatlands of Alberta.

We settle back, satisfied Dad has responded. I stare out the window, wondering why on earth anyone would need so much wheat.

"It seems almost a shame to eat them. They look so peaceful," says my Mom.

It's growing dark as Sinatra signs off "… *in my heart you will remain. My stardust melody. The memory of love's refrain.*"

My father snaps on the headlights. "Sheena, give me a cigarette. I'm out."

"I don't have any. You must have them."

"You opened a carton this morning. They must be in your purse."

"They're not in…"

"Just look, would you."

I can see the moon rising, balanced above the crimson farewell of a dying sun.

Beside me, my brother's struggles to free himself from the hated seat, always heated, become Herculean. A tiny hand bashes against my shoulder.

I turn and sneer. "Lose your car?"

His face is blue.

"Dad, there's something wrong with David!"

Wary eyes widen in the rearview, and the car slams to a stop. My mother plunges over the backseat, tearing my brother from his belt, her face savaged by fear. She holds him upside down by one leg, and he swings in pop-eyed shudders, dying right in front of me.

"He's choking!"

My father slams his hand against my brother's back. Flat blows echo as Dad pounds at the frantic pendulum and David's face contorts in an airless shriek.

A desperate punch, full force from my father, and a tiny car door shoots from my brother's throat and onto the seat.

And I knew — as my brother sputtered and wept, and my mother soothed and caressed, and my father massaged his hand and fumbled for cigarettes, as trucks pulled past and the stars brightened on those endless fields and I recovered my car and clutched it to my chest — that nothing would ever change and we would all be together forever.

▶

When I told my four-year-old son I was leaving, that I was moving out of our house, and that I wouldn't always be there all the time any more, I cupped his face to comfort him.

It was like laying my hands on heaven just so I could scratch out the stars.

Penumbra

X/Y. A chromosome joke—the yellowed sign above the inset buttons, in that hallway between two locked doors. X for the women's ward, Y for the men's. But I have not been here, or even in Canada, for close to half a year, and that part of my brain where Grade 10 Biology resides has slipped into the trough of unneeded information. I hit the wrong button, buzzing Male instead of Female.

And I know I've made a mistake almost immediately because the buzz brings a cry from behind the door beside me on my left. Hoarse, insistent, and unmistakably a man's. Unintelligible, yet in its rhythm approaching what was once a word, the voice is full of rage and the sudden pained reminder of a large and wider world. I listen, push the other button and wait.

▶

It's 1969, and all of us gathered in that small apartment in Calgary are straining our eyes, trying to make out something significant from the pocked black and white pictures scrolling across the television screen. My parents and their friends are quiet now, eyes and ears intent on image and commentary, glasses of wine untouched. They sit frozen in ray and flicker, stirring only to hiss an occasional "shush" at the small boy crouched on the carpet beside the couch. Neil Armstrong is about to walk on the moon and I have the hiccups.

Like the lunar voyage, my hiccups have lasted an eternity and I can tell from the increasingly irritated glances of the grownups that I'm about one more diaphragm shudder from expulsion. Hic. It comes. And I am out. My mother gathers me up, and, brushing off protests with whispers and kisses touched with soft perfume, leaves me alone in my bedroom, well away from the Age of Aquarius and the march of history.

I lie there on my bed for a few minutes, crying and hiccing in the low illumination of the room. Then with the slow realization of exactly where that light is coming from, stand up on my mattress, draw back the curtains from the small window above, and stare at the bright face of the full moon, filled with the absolute certainty that if I only look long enough I will see those men moving on its surface.

▸

The cries have stopped now. Presumably calmed by the same nurse who has just given me a short course on genetic structure and the quick assurance that someone from the women's ward will be with me "right away." Anxious, I pace the floor in an alphabet loop, from X to Y and back again, filling the stretched minutes of the short delay with the lazy dip of memory.

▸

All along the harbour small bulbs nod in cheerful anticipation, occasionally breaking into zigzag traces that echo silent struggles and a slow pull toward the water's surface.

Night fishing in Portovenere.

This is where I have come—almost every evening—on the last leg of my Italian tour. I drive up the coast from La Spezia to get a cappuccino and stroll the cobblestone passages between the ocean and the snaggletooth arc of pastel-coloured apartments that make up the front of the fishing village: I move past noisy cafés, alley cats, all the brightly coloured dories drying on the shore, and up to the end of the peninsula.

At the end, there are crumbling steps and a banded-slate slope where a Romanesque church resides and the blue expanse of the Mediterranean begins. Just outside the church's ruined courtyard there is a huge seaside grotto, and I climb down into the cavern to sit close to the sea, surrounded by shadow and an ocean that extends forever. And held in arms of water and stone I stare out at the distance, at moon and endless horizon.

▸

X opens and an attendant smiles me through. "We haven't seen you here for a while," she says.

"I've been travelling."

Unlike much of the rest of Riverview Hospital, the visiting room in Unit 8X attempts an escape from utilitarianism, achieving with its high-backed chairs and brightly coloured prints the generic familiarity of a lobby at a Motel 6. At the moment, a couple of the chairs are occupied by a pair of opposites: one an old woman, dentureless and silent; the other young, toothy, gibbering.

"Yes, I know," she says in response to nothing said. "I've always known that."

The third woman in the room—a well-preserved red-head—has her own special chair: one with locking wheels, a reclining back, and an adjustable food tray. It is covered in dark brown leatherette and resembles nothing so much as a portable dentist's chair. Unlike the other two patients, the redhead is strapped into her chair with a stained harness that fits between her legs and around her hips like a diaper. The harness is slightly loose, and whenever the woman strains to free herself, which she does every few minutes, it gathers up a few centimetres of skirt, exposing blue veins and bruises running the length of her legs.

I touch her. "Hi, Mom," I say.

"BobBobBob . . ." she starts, stuttering out my father's name.

▶

About twenty minutes is all I can take. When I visit. Twenty minutes of feeding her grapes, seeing her stare, and ducking the slaps and scratches that slash out for no reason. And of watching the Alzheimer's, the disease that's ravaged my mother for the last six years, and learning once again that, in the end, what it finally takes away is you. After a while, all that's left is a familiar skin encasing something alien. A crumbling husk around a creeping unknown, and any truly human contact becomes as impossible as seeing Neil Armstrong walking on the moon with your naked eye.

But there are times, and they are very few, when something lucid slips from my mother's lips, like a loose photo from a family album: a name, a sentence, a sliver of memory. And it is then that I tell my mother that I am not so far from her. That I have an inkling of what it's like to be behind her eyes; to be caught in a world of shadow; to be held in a half-lit cavern staring out at the dim horizon of an unfamiliar sea.

Neither Here nor There

I 've only been mugged once. An interesting experience that ended up with the both of us too exhausted to do anything more than treat the other as a human being. He got my leather coat, and I got my credit cards returned with a hug of approval. A bit Iron-Johnish that last bit, but at least we both avoided jail. Which is just as well, as I've never had the desire to go to prison.

I did attend high school though: a vile waste of time from which I gained nothing but a pathological loathing of the classroom and some skill at getting out of bad situations.

Although I might have inherited this talent from my father, who managed to escape both Scotland and the dread routine of National Service. Instead of heading into the army, he grabbed my mother and ran off to the Caribbean where they rented motorcycles and plotted a future in Canada. I like to think of my parents this way: tanned and barefoot on the ledge of the future.

They stopped in Hamilton in 1959. Some time after that I was born (in 1963) and some time after that I fell down a flight of stairs, creating my first memory.

Next, we moved to Calgary, where my new brother con-
tinued a family tradition and found his own steps, concussing
himself and dislodging his own early memories.

Finally, 1970, and Vancouver, where we lived in a hotel
on English Bay, and I discovered beaches, elevators, and the
miracle of room service.

Lotus Land at seven and a half.

Or at least this is the way I remember it. My Dad disagrees
with most of the salient points of this short family history,
although we do agree that I was, in fact, born. After all,
we've got the paperwork, even though the exact year of my
commencement is becoming less certain the longer I live. My
birth certificate states 1963, but B.C. bureaucrats insist I was
born a year earlier, and emblazoned this belief across my
driver's license, effectively fictionalizing me when I received
my license at the age of eighteen. I no longer care much
either way, and simply flip a mental coin when filling out
D.O.B. requests. Youth is overrated, and I'm happy to be as
old as you need me to be.

Even without the confusion of bureaucratic edicts, it's
always taken a certain amount of head-math to figure out
exactly how old I am. December babies generally dawdle in
the age race, their birthdays last-minute affairs tacked onto the
festivities of Christmas. Our years always seem longer, our
contemporaries just that little bit older. Growing up, my school
friends would shoot into their next year, barging past age
barriers and into adolescence, cars, and girlfriends seemingly

eons ahead of me. Their birthdays were singular spring, summer, and autumn celebrations, while mine were more like afterthoughts, silver medals in the sprint towards adulthood.

Now that I've reached a sort of adulthood, I'm more surprised by birthdays than anything else, shaken by time's swift passage and the advent of another annual survey of goals accomplished and undone. And as I grow older, I find myself increasingly concerned with memory, something that's not particularly surprising given my family history and genetics' cruel twists.

My mother was just verging on her sixties when Alzheimer's snuck up on her. It was hard to tell something was going wrong at first. She was always a bit eccentric—always a bit absent-minded, prone to endlessly cheerful chit-chat and constant requests for tea. My brother and I had long ago learned to tune most of it out, so it's more than possible we just didn't pay attention.

Until the tomatoes, that is.

Can after can filling up cupboards. Every shopping trip brought home new tins, with my mother insisting she needed them for some special dish that never appeared. Then there were all the misplaced items, things like keys and glasses, all shrugged off easily enough, except that it kept happening. Almost every day. After that, there was the accident—she became confused at an intersection and racked up her car on some railway tracks. Next, she couldn't tell time. Or do simple arithmetic. Talk without repeating every second sentence. And then, not so quickly that she wasn't horribly aware that something really bad was happening, but far too fast for the rest of us . . . well . . . she just wasn't.

Some people's birthdays are all about making lifetime memories. Mine are all about forgetting. Nowadays, I like to use my birthdays to check in on what's missing, to take stock of the vast array of things I no longer recall: what's-her-name, for example. Or that actor in that movie, you know, the one with the spaceship and the musical lights. I can't recollect how to change a spark plug, who the Fathers of Confederation were, how stagflation occurs or why Lester Pearson was important. Grade 4 is gone, as are the rules for Monopoly, and my current postal code. The purpose of a logarithm and my grandmother's first name. Like most people, the details of my formal education vanished long ago. The course listings in faded transcripts spark as much recognition as Aramaic: Introduction to Micro-Economics? Huh? Communication as a Social and Biological Function? Who dat? And that was me who wrote those essays? I knew that? No way.

I don't recall 1998 at all either.

The bulk of this stuff doesn't matter, of course. Most of it's trivial, and the rest I can look up on the internet (used to solve equations in which exponents are unknown, logarithms and their scales are often used to plot basic physical and biological processes, the Richter scale, for example . . . Canada's 14th

Prime Minister, Lester Pearson won the Nobel Peace Prize in 1957 . . . Richard Dreyfuss . . . thanks, Google). But as I hurtle towards my own possible first date with early onset Alzheimer's, I take some comfort in the notion that what we remember is, in some ways, nothing really at all. At least in the conventional way most of us think about memory.

We're all pretty much wrong when it comes to memory: wrong both in the veracity of our recollections, and in our perception of how memory actually functions. Most of us think of memory as a type of mental Rolodex with our histories and carefully acquired bits of knowledge filed neatly inside. Need something from the past? Scroll through the cards, and pull out the one that's appropriate.

And while this may be somewhat true for simple facts, there's mounting evidence that memory isn't simply a passive storage system, but rather a process much more analogous to a web page created dynamically when we enter a request, a kind of mental Google search (thanks again, big guy). Past events don't really exist until we put in a topic and pull it all together from everything we've ever experienced. As we change, so do our memories. Literally. Present prejudices, simple fictions, and our entire sums of knowledge shape the shards of our pasts. From this perspective, recall resembles the ultimate *MacGyver*: whole lives spontaneously cobbled together with cognitive duct tape and the Swiss Army knife of learned behaviour. Memories are handyman specials, full of flaws.

I don't know about you—of course—but this sounds suspiciously like the craft of fiction to me. It makes memory into yet another art form, a generative activity, where every old memory is always made anew. The very process of retrieving a memory not only creates but also changes that recollection forever. Heisenberg would have loved this notion. Apparently James Frey would as well. Tapes aside, Nixon obviously had a tooth-sucking grasp of it, and it looks like the Bushes live by it. I have no idea how Stephen Harper regards this, since, like many Canadians, I've never heard him speak in public, but I'm certain it'll serve him well. Maybe it has already. I really don't recall.

Like politicians, we're all unreliable narrators. All of us creative artists subject to time, bias, and wishful thinking regarding our personal pasts.

Take your first memory, for example. Is it yours? Or did someone tell it to you? I know mine's a muddle. It took place in Hamilton, another place I can't picture at all (from all accounts a good thing). I do remember stairs, tumbling strobes of black and white as I thudded down steps, and a small galaxy of pain — I recollect the pain pretty well. I recall being lifted and soothed, but not by whom, and seeing the ceiling scroll by before being set down on what seemed like a soft and endless green expanse. Yet unless I had a brief moment of toddler astral projection, unless I had a long-lost ability to stand outside my own body, I know this first memory simply can't be true. The problem is that when I conjure up this small misadventure, what I see is me. There I am—fat, happy, slightly bruised—lying on a blanket in the middle of a ping-pong table. Somehow someone's yarn stuck and became my own story.

Still, this *is* my first memory, all of it, both on the table and looking back at myself. I swear it's true. I can see it, right there, right behind my eyes. It's as clear as the year I was born.

My mother's still alive, still hanging in there close to ten years after "Penumbra" was first published. Doesn't speak, doesn't walk, and eats only when prompted: place a spoon to her cheek and she'll mouth at the food. She sleeps much of the day, but I don't know if she dreams. The best I can hope is that she's floating in some safe and timeless la-la land, in her own sea of green, so to speak.

Ten years have also diminished my own memories of her. I find it harder to recall exactly what my mom was like when she was well: how she walked, laughed, spoke—"Jimmy, I think a cup of tea would be lovely right now." The memories are there, but faded, tinged with nostalgia's dim glow and the flat reminder of photo albums. They've become suspect, tainted by time, uncertainty, and the anecdotes of others. They're there, but less so. She's less present. Less reliable. More and more like something I just made up.

We'll Always Have Hiroshima

G ina saw everything through the end of the world. An apocalyptic tickertape ran just underneath the surface of her eyes, turning everything outside into an endless Nagasaki.

"Will there...*Heat*...be fries...*Blast*...with that?...*Fire.*"

She made this small confession between bites of special sauce on a mostly unauthorized excursion to the McDonalds across the street from the centre. And, finally, I understood something about her that had bothered me over the few months I had known her: a habit she had of covering her mouth when she laughed or smiled. At first I thought it was bad teeth. Next, simple shyness. But now I knew why the hand went over the hole—it was to keep the horror in.

▶

"Number ten: there are no such things as right or wrong feelings!"

This was my favourite part of our small morning mantra, and I would yell it out with the pop-eyed enthusiasm of an

Amway Double Diamond preaching to the as-yet-unconverted, garnering undisguised amusement from rest of the group and eye-narrowed irritation from the staff. Both reactions were, of course, okay.

In actuality I liked the entire mantra: I liked the regularity and rhythm of the chanted mumble of symptoms and self-affirmations sliding off twenty coffee-thickened tongues—it was soothing and helped cut the caffeine. But the only part I truly listened to was the last. I listened because it freed me from responsibility.

Mornings were a delicate time for me, and I would always choose my eight a.m. neighbours carefully, closely scanning their faces to determine disorders and medication levels in order to complement my needs. Schizophrenics for energy and oblique conversation, depressives for bleak tranquility and stony calm.

Today I was sitting beside Bob.

All I knew about Bob, all anyone knew about Bob, and this was from our obligatory first-day symptom description, was that he was recovering from a triple addiction: cigarettes, alcohol, and painkillers. Since volunteering this information, he had withdrawn into a silence so profound most of us had honestly forgotten he could communicate at all, and simply regarded him as something to be sat beside when you couldn't quite live up to the demands of light conversation. Thus I was a bit too startled to actually understand when Bob shifted his head out of its perpetual slump and rumbled something at me.

"Pardon?" I said.

"I said what the fuck is wrong with you man? Why are you so fucking happy? I mean, what exactly are you doing here?"

I paused for an answer and Bob's head sank back into its slump.

"I'm here," I said into his bald spot, "because nobody ever told me about number ten."

▶

"So what, did I retard myself? I drank a lot . . . I think I retarded myself."

The chair leather squeaked as the doctor crossed his legs.

"You're not listening to me," he said. "You're not retarded, you're depressed. I told you, you're depressed."

"Of course I'm depressed! I can't think, I can't make decisions and I haven't slept for three days . . . Oh, christ, tears. Fucking tears. I haven't cried since I was twelve."

"There're some tissues on the table. Now I know this is hard for you, but I want you to listen to me very carefully. You're not just unhappy, you're clinically depressed. It's an illness. It was triggered by your mother's health problems, and there was nothing you could do about it."

"Oh, great, I'm crazy."

"You're not crazy, and you're not retarded. You're sick. You have a chemical imbalance. That's why you can't sleep, and that's why you can't make decisions."

"But why can't I think? I study English and I can't even read the newspaper."

"It's part of the same thing. Your concentration is slow. And you can think. Look at that print over there and tell me what you see."

I look up at the painting on the wall opposite me. A woman in a ditch. Nice dress.

"The drowning of Ophelia. Pre-Raphaelite."

"Very good. Most people wouldn't know that."

"Yeah, I failed a class in it once."

The doctor made a note in his pad and looked back up at me.

"I'm going to ask you a question," he said, "and I want you to be very honest with me. Have you been thinking about killing yourself?"

▶

STANFORD NORTH DAY CENTRE
Daily Schedule

9:00	Roll Call, Duty Assignment and Affirmations
9:30	Psycho-Drama and Social Interaction Skills
10:30	Free Time and Coffee
11:00	Art and Craft Therapy
12:00	LUNCH
1:00	Self-Assertion Techniques and Disorder Information Sessions

2:30   Free Time and Coffee
3:00   Badminton!

No one will play badminton with me. I've discovered that the mentally ill are often in poor condition and lack self-esteem: they don't have the physical and mental stamina to stand up to the one badminton shot I've mastered—a vicious return shot that bullets the birdie right between my opponent's eyes. Simple enough to deflect if you've got the speed and the balls to stand up to it. But no one else is as far along in their self-assertion course as I am.

The only person who I can ever get a game with now is Gina. And that's because I simply can't muster up the killer instinct to try and take her head off. She's so awkward and graceless at the game, it'd be like shooting a new-born Bambi. Instead, I feed her long arcing lobs, popping the birdies high up towards the yellowed fluorescents of the aging gym; hitting them just right, with just enough force to give them a half-second hesitation at the top of their trip: a small rest stop before they slowly turn and plunge straight down in a gathering fall—like something dropped from the Enola Gay.

▶

Bottom is a lot deeper than you think it is. And there is, on the descent, a kind of panicked fascination as you keep plummeting past what you thought was ground zero. Eventually, the fascination ends and you find yourself . . . somewhere . . . down too deep, drowning in an ocean no one else can see.

▶

"Meow, Meow, Meow." I am a cat. And I will remain a cat until I can make someone laugh. Then they will become a cat and I'll be allowed to get off my hands and knees, sit back on my chair and rejoin my own species. Stuff like this happens a lot in our social interaction sessions. I hope one day they'll let me bark.

But right now I'm being made to meow at Flo—a borderline psychotic street-person whose most attractive habit is chain-smoking—and it looks like my chances of moving up the evolutionary scale are slim. She simply stares at me with an impassive face and slightly unfocussed eyes. She looks more bored than anything else, and I'm certain she's seen this all before.

I decide to try to at least get her attention.

"Hey Flo," I say, "tune in, would ya. Meow, fuckin' meow."

"Billy!" It's Rose, our interpersonal trainer. "You know the rules, cats can't speak."

"Yeah, well they don't humiliate themselves either."

Rose pauses as she tries to find the right words to fit into the formula for constructive criticism: "When you do_____, it makes me feel_____, so please try not to_____ anymore."

Flo's eyes are starting to focus.

"When you use sarcasm, it makes me feel insulted, so please try not to do . . . uh . . . it anymore," says Rose.

"Try 'derision' or maybe 'ridicule'," I suggest with a helpful smile.

"Pardon me?"

"As a synonym for 'sarcasm'. Of course you'll have to change the infinitive, but it should fit."

Rose's glasses flash danger, catching the light as she leans towards me. Obviously, I haven't given the right response.

She looks at me expectantly for a few seconds, wipes her glasses for dramatic effect, then digs into a long lecture about the need for consideration and the importance of others' feelings.

But I'm no longer listening. Instead I'm focussed on an internal monotone: an anger, vast and inappropriate, one degree away from rage. It's a feeling I'm familiar with, and I clamp down, shut off . . . separate, anything to stop the explosion . . . the exposure . . . the regret.

I stare into the carpet, frozen.

The sound of phlegm surging towards decayed teeth. Flo is laughing.

"Whassa matter," she rasps. "Cat got your tongue? Cat got your tongue? Cat got your —"

▶

Gina was late today. Didn't arrive until almost lunch. In tears. Fired from her part-time job at Taco Bell. I tried to find out what had happened, but couldn't get through the moat of counselors around her, the flood of emotional support that islanded her for the rest of the day. Decided to give her a call at home later on, but remembered too late that I didn't know her number. Or her last name.

Gina is my closest friend in this place.

▶

". . . depression doesn't just refer to a feeling of unhappiness. The key to the disorder is in the word itself. De-press. To push down. Most depressives have learned, almost instinctively from childhood, to hold down their emotional selves. It's a way of freeing themselves from the intensity of emotion, especially anger or pain . . ."

I must be getting better, because I can feel my inner self. And my inner self is bored.

The novelty of being crazy has pretty much worn off by now, thirteen weeks into this program. Routine and rote have taken the place of discovery, especially in this, our Disorder Information Sessions, which have always smacked of the classroom and now feel like midterms in November.

Besides, the lecture we're listening to at the moment has segued from depression into schizophrenia, and that lies well outside my own particular pathological interest.

Flo is interested though. But I strongly suspect that she's on a different channel than the rest of us since she's writing at least ten words for every one the lecturer utters, with every alternating sentence in a different colour pen. I sneak a peek into her notebook: a tie-dye version of Linear B.

"Mrrphh mrrph mrrrph Billy?"

A question from my left. Gopinder is trying to make contact with me again.

Theoretically, Gopinder is my responsibility. As part of our rehabilitative road back into normal society, each one of us gets a charge—a new admittant into the program—to take care of until they get comfortable enough to find coffee, food, washrooms, and badminton racquets for themselves. Most people get their first charge after seven weeks. I got Gopinder after ten.

Unfortunately, although I am more than happy to show Gopinder the ropes and racquets of this place, I haven't, as yet, been able to make out one word he's said to me beyond my name. Gopinder's self-esteem is so low that he's afraid to commit to anything intelligible, on the off chance that he might make a challengeable assertion, like "the weather is nice today" or "this food is good." And a challenge is some-thing Gopinder just can't handle at the moment—it would probably send him into a straitjacket.

But I don't want to ignore Gopinder's attempts to be a human being, god knows he's had enough of that, so I always try to answer him. Usually by category. Always by non sequitur. Last week, it was short personal anecdotes. This week, historical trivia.

"Yes, it's true, Gopinder," I answer his mrrph. "Gandhi

did share his bed with two virgins every night. It was a test of his vow of celibacy."

Gopinder beams and nods rapidly, lemur eyes shining with the excitement of acknowledgement.

"Mrrph, mrrph," he says.

I mrrph back at him then turn and slouch even further in my chair, idly looking around the semicircle of seats gathered around the speaker and making a mental inventory of just who's MIA today:

Richard: Bi-polar disorder, uncontrollable rages, spousal abuse. Occasionally thinks that he's Jesus when he's manic. Once got arrested for stealing cheese.

Virginia: Episodic depression lately triggered by a long, drawn-out divorce. Grabbed all the pillows in her house and nested in her basement for three months until someone finally came and got her. Ordered pizza every day she was down there. Pepperoni.

Doug: Cartoonist by trade, chronic depressive by temperament. Very funny, but hasn't got a chance in hell of ever getting syndicated, since he always kills off his main character by the third or fourth panel—usually by suicide.

Pam: Dietitian. Schizophrenic.

Rory: Art teacher.

James, Rachael, most of the affectives. Gina.

I know where the MIAs are. They're all up in the High Room. The small room on the second floor of the building that houses the Day program. The High Room is where intensive group therapy goes on, where the staff gets out their Freudian shovels and tries to dig down into the roots of people's disorders. Lots of stuff about Mom and Dad, and the death of the family dog. It's the place where all the Kleenexes are kept, and each of us, after a certain point, is given the option of skipping the Information Sessions and going up there instead.

I will not go to the High Room.

"Okay that's enough for today. It's coffee time everyone. Remember next week we're having a quiz, so make sure you know the four D's of depression, and the seven warning signs of schizophrenia . . . uh, Flo, you can stop writing. The lesson's over now."

I grab Gopinder and head over to the coffee machine. We chat briefly—"Henry Ford was an anti-Semite and an early admirer of Hitler's National Socialist party. I don't know the range of his prejudices though, since you could only get the Model T in black"—and then I point him in the direction of the pool table as I head out the side door, into the smoking area, to try and find Gina.

▸

She's been crying, of course. Everybody cries in and after the High Room. It's part of the catharsis, supposedly. All I know is that everybody seems a lot less happy coming out

than going in. I give her a light, and then lead her away from
the rest of the smokers, to a picnic table just around the side
of the building, to the place we always go.

"Would you?" she asks.

"C'mon, Gina, you know you don't have to ask."

I lay my hands upon her shoulders.

High Room recovery massage is our small ritual. A private
affair between Gina and me, a time for her to try and make
some sense of what just went on. I perch on the picnic table,
as she sits on the bench below, turned away from me and
talking as my fingers trace the muscles of her neck, shoulders, back; arms falling into the rhythm of our conversation.

"I was in the hot seat today," she says. "I talked about my
father."

"That's a surprise," I reply. "I didn't realize our parents
had anything to do with our problems."

Her hand goes up to her face. She's laughing. I always
make her laugh. I think it's why she trusts me.

"I don't know why I started talking about him. I mean, I've
always loved my father, and he's always looked after me the
best he could. But I realized when I started talking about him,
just how angry I was at him . . . at his expectations . . . and just
how afraid I've been to show that anger, ever since I've been
a little girl."

The hand goes over the hole.

She falls silent, dragging on her cigarette, grey smoke
wreathing raven hair; a mushroom cloud over a blackened

city; shadows trapped in cement. I rub her spine and push my palms a little harder, trying to free tight muscles.

She stubs out her cigarette. "Billy... why won't you go to the High Room? It'd be nice to have you there."

"Forget it. No way. You'd have to kill me first."

"I know, but why? It's not that bad you know."

"I'm not gonna go because . . ."

. . . because you of all people should know. Look at you, you're twenty-one and you've been through this program three times already. You've spent half your life lying on couches paying strangers to listen to you, to tell you what to do, and you're not any better. And you'll never get any better if you keep heading up to places like the High Room because you're going in the wrong direction. You've got to go out, not in. And you should know that, the clues are there; they've always been there, right inside your eyes and you just don't see . . . you just don't see that it's all about . . . it's all about Hiroshima . . . it's all about Nagasaki . . . Los Alamos, and the first time for everything. When Oppenheimer and his crew were lying out in that desert, watching that damn thing go off, they sure as hell weren't thinking about classical Indian literature, that "I am become death" shit, that's a fucking dinnertime story Oppenheimer came up with so he could still eat after he became a security risk. You know what they were thinking when they saw that big cloud shoot up into that empty sky, they were thinking "thank god it stopped" because they didn't fucking know. The whole time they worked on that project, even when they pushed that button, they were dealing with the possibility that the chain reaction wouldn't stop; that the explosion couldn't be contained and that the whole damn universe would go up in one blinding flash of light, and they pushed it anyhow . . . and that's what these guys do to you, Gina. They find your button and they push it down and they keep it down, and you're left with what's left, which is nothing but a stuck button and no idea where it's going to end, while they go home to dinner . . .

". . . I'm not gonna go because Flo would miss me, Gina." She laughs again and we sit there for a while in comfortable silence as I keep on massaging her back: hands casting calls to the surface. Taps on aquarium glass. Soft signals to down below, telling her to come away from what's inside, and find a moment of silence on Armistice Day.

▶

Week seventeen and my counselor thinks I should try socializing in the evenings again, instead of hanging around at home watching TV or reading. I think I'll follow his advice. I think I'll go get drunk.

▶

"CLUNK . . . when you throw . . . CLUNK . . . beer in my face . . . CLUNK . . . you make me feel . . . CLUNK . . . angry."

CLUNK. "Angry."

CLUNK. "Angry."

In self-assertion circles this is known as the broken-record technique: a simple repetition of your position until your co-communicant understands both your situation and your emotions. The clunking, the sound the guy's head makes as I bounce it off the bar, is my own innovation, and I am quite certain that it will help speed the process of mutual understanding.

I stop for a second to check his progress—dumb beast eyes squint around my fingers. He tries to throw a punch.

"Oh no you don't." CLUNK. "Angry."

CLUNK. "Angry."

A quick emotional-state survey.

"I feel that you felt annoyed when your girlfriend stuck her tongue down my throat. Is this how you felt?"

He spits out some blood. "Stop man, I give okay, just let me up."

"That wasn't the question . . ." I begin, but rough hands grab my shoulders and pull me away from him.

"Okay, buddy, you're out."

I can see the exit sign rapidly approaching and I try to establish an interpersonal connection one final time as I'm dragged though a sea of half-amused faces.

"When you throw me out it makes me feel like I've blown my cover charge, so please don't throw me out."

The door slams shut behind me.

▸

"... and how did this bar fight make you feel?" the doctor asks.

"Good. It made me feel ... really, really ... uh ... happy, especially since I got a chance to use the things you guys taught me. In fact, I think I'm cured. You can't be depressed if you feel happy, right?"

They want me to stay in the program for a few extra weeks.

So much for number ten.

▸

It's graduation day and Doug the Depressed Cartoonist has drawn me a certificate of sanity, complete with the date, time, and a fake Seal of Approval from C. Everett Koop, the former Surgeon General of the United States. "Billy is sane," reads the balloon coming out of C. Everett's mouth.

The certificate has an excellent likeness of me bursting out of a straitjacket with everyone else on the staff and the group standing around applauding. Doug's even included himself, something that is truly surprising since he's confessed to a loathing of self-portraiture: a tiny man hanging from a tree well in the background. It looks like the rope wasn't quite long enough to snap the suicide's neck and the man is kicking his legs in the agony of slow asphyxiation. I'm a little worried about Doug.

"Thank you, Doug, this must have taken a lot of work."

"Turn it over," he says. "Take a look at the back."

I flip the card over, and I see small notes of thanks, good wishes, and hopes for contact and friendship in the future. The card is covered with addresses and phone numbers, and everyone has written.

"I . . . I don't what to say . . . uh . . . Gopinder, I can't read your handwriting. Flo, this phone number only has four digits, maybe you'd better phone me instead . . . um, thank you so much everyone. I can't say how much you all . . . I can't tell you how grateful I am to all of you, how much you've helped me understand . . . I promise I'll keep in touch with every single one of you . . ."

I stammer to a halt and look at them, and I see the affection in their eyes, and I know if I keep talking I'm going to cry. And I think I'm going to cry anyhow, so I look down at the floor to hide my eyes, until a small hand fits itself into mine, and I look up into Gina's eyes and the perfect teeth of a wide and open smile.

▸

I never try to contact any of them again.

▸

"Billy! Billy!"

Oh, christ. Not here. Not now. Don't let this be happening.

"Billy, it's me, Gina! Remember, from the Day Program?"

Her voice is too loud, like a deaf person trying to whisper in a library. Everyone in the movie theatre is watching us she moves from her seat and up the aisle to greet me.

"Oh, hi, Gina. What's it been...six months? You look good."

Actually she doesn't. Her face has broken out and her eyes are clouded. A half-grin is plastered on her face and through it I see yellowed teeth. I shift my popcorn and awkwardly shake her hand.

"Thanks, so do you." She looks at me expectantly.

"Oh, Gina, this is Laura. Laura, this is Gina, an old friend of mine."

Gina sniggers. "More like cell-mates, you mean. Nice to meet you, Laura. So, Billy, have you been back to the Day Program? I haven't been back since they finally gave me a diagnosis. Turns out I'm a borderline, you know, a psychotic."

Laura's welcoming smile cements into place as her eye-brows shoot toward her hairline. Shit. That's it. I really liked Laura too.

"Yeah," Gina continues, blithely unaware of all the heads swivelled in her direction. "That's where all those bombs we're coming from. I don't have 'em now. The medication cleared that up. Are you still taking stuff?"

Shuttup. Shuttup. Shuttup. Please, shut up.

"Well, that's really good Gina. I'm happy for you. Anyhow, it looks like the movie is going to start soon, so we better get some seats. Um...I'll talk to you after the movie, okay?"

"Okay, I'll be waiting for you. Nice meeting you, Laura."

Laura and I head to some seats in silence. Blessedly, the film, some Schwarzenegger kill-fest, starts up just as we sit, and conversation becomes, not impossible, but at least avoidable for the time being, giving me time to think of what to say as the body count begins.

I debate strategies for about a half an hour, but the weight of unasked questions is just too much for me to be imaginative and I decide to try and go with honesty.

I lean toward her ear. "Look, Laura, maybe we better talk, huh?"

"I don't see what we have to talk about. I mean we've been seeing each other for over three months, and you never bothered to tell me that you had that . . . sort of problem. I thought I knew you."

Arnold blows somebody's head off. Big laughs from the audience.

"You do know me. It's just that . . . I can't talk about this here. Let's go outside. Please."

A pause, a nod, and we start making our way out, tripping over feet and "excuse me"s. Laura deftly slides by the fat man on the aisle and is out the door, as I get entangled in the elephant dance of his feet.

"Christ, move it, I can't see!" he snarls in a loud voice, and heads turn as something explodes up on the screen and the theatre fills with the bright illumination of a slow-motion inferno. And as I stumble past the man, I look at the screen, and as I look, my eyes sweep the audience...and I can see her. I can see her looking back at me, and her hand is clasped across her mouth, and as I turn and walk up the aisle, away from the flame, from the slow spread of fire, I can hear the sound of something dying.

We Will Be Landing

"The Blue Danube" drifts through my headphones, lulling me into a small escape and the promise of happier times. Sleep, the gold-medal goal of any international flight, seems almost in reach, and I settle back in my seat, letting the river carry me away from the grueling confines of economy class and steerage in the sky.

A heavy thud on my right armrest. Another on the left. My seat shakes with the turbulent deposit of an extra 180 pounds, heart beating an angry counterpoint to Strauss's naff tinkle as my headrest bounces with the awkward and now familiar grasp of inebriated hands. I open my eyes and stare into an abyss of acid-washed denim. It's back again, my boon companion on this endless voyage: the Scottish crotch.

The Scot—I'd immediately forgotten his name after the polite nicety of quick introductions five or six hours ago— lurches onto his seat, twirling awkwardly as he bangs himself back into place by the window, then deftly pulls out

the beer can he'd stuffed into the seat pocket before his brief
excursion. The unpopped top of another can glints from the
dim recesses of the distended pouch, threatening a future
bathroom break and another unsteady exhibition of armrest
gymnastics.

"Och no, no need to get up," he burred the first time he
hunched his way across our seats and out into the aisle. "You
just stay put, and I'll go over instead. I dinna want to disturb
you."

I glance over at my wife on the aisle seat beside me,
wanting indignant commiseration, but she is happily asleep
and has been for hours.

I hate her for this.

I turn my attention back to the window seat. The Scot
gulps a quick swig from the can, red face floating above an
orange Irn-Bru T-shirt. He had been drinking Coors but
now the stewardesses are feeding him some blue–and-white
off-brand whose logo is buried beneath stubby fingers. He
notices me watching, mouths something, then grins and
mimes at me to remove my phones.

I unshackle myself from the in-flight music station.

He gestures vaguely towards the back of the plane. "I've
found," he says happily, "a secret place to smoke. You should
come join me."

Visions of Air Marshals dance through my head. "I don't
think we're allowed to do that here. Where's the secret place,
anyhow…the washroom? They've got smoke detectors in
there. We'll get caught for sure."

"No, no, not the bathroom. It's close to there though—it's a secret place. C'mon, I'll show you."

I hesitate, caught between fear and need, nicotine-starved cells screaming assent, common sense calmly stating the opposite. Mostly his accent spurs some primordial streak of Presbyterian self-denial. I'd enjoy sneaking a smoke, so I'd better not do it. God will punish me for it—just as I'm sure this flight is celestial payback for some small transgression on my part. Jaywalking, perhaps. Or skipping Sunday services for thirty-seven years.

Instead, I give the Scot the vacant promise I make to myself on every long flight. "No, no thanks, I'm trying to use this trip as a chance to quit."

He shrugs. "Suit yourself," then plugs himself into the seatback monitor and the fraudulent brogue of Shrek.

Constant armrest hopping aside, the Scot's been pretty good as drunks go. Decidedly not garrulous, thank god, except for a short stint of chitchat after the first few beers. He talked a bit about his recent travels in the U.S., and I established my Scottish credentials, explaining that my mom and dad were from Sauchie and Rothesay respectively. A faint air of disapproval emanated from him at the mention of my father's hometown, Rothesay, a place that spent a fair bit of its recent history as a resort destination. Obviously nobody of any serious import could have possibly come from a town where people attempted to have fun. He brightened up, though, at the news of our mutual nicotine addiction, gratified we were upholding the Gaelic tradition of shared suffering.

After that, there wasn't much talk from him. Mostly muttered grumbles about no-smoking policies and requests for more beer from the frozen-grin stewardesses who hovered around our section of the plane. His acrobatics had caught their attention pretty quickly, and they were determined to keep him as placated as possible, stretching out liquor deliveries as long as they could without pissing him off, whispering apologies in his frequent absences.

"It's okay," I'd answer. "It's really, really, just fine."

And it was. I honestly meant it. I could forgive the Scot almost anything in his search for sanctuary, comfort, and the fulfillment of simple human needs. I understood this: hell, I'd been to the promised land once before—bumped up to business class on British Airways due to overbooking and divine intervention—so I know all of this is feasible and that it lies just up there behind class lines and that mysterious curtain. I know there's legroom and freshly squeezed juice and hot towels and solicitous service and food with at least some taste, and that we all deserve these simple pleasures and not stale bags of salty pretzel chunks. Go ahead and get what you need, as much as possible, especially if it's free, and particularly if it drags you out of the oblivion of air travel and into a better place of your own devising.

Above and beyond all that, I feel I owe you understanding. Not only will you be the person I die next to when the plane goes down, but I also have a genetic obligation to tolerate you as family of a sort, as a species of fellow flying Scotsman. Chances are that we are related somewhere down the genealogical trough, given Highlanders' reputations for solitary walks and insular breeding patterns. At the very least, it's likely our clans tried to massacre each other at some point in our Motherland's depressingly violent history. So we do share that bond. And it's not as if I haven't been in the same position as you before, sotted and suffering as an interminable plane trip drags on to an ever-receding conclusion.

►

There comes a point in just about every journey where nothing really matters. After all the nail-biting prep, the nervous nitpicking, list-checking, reserving, and packing, after the meat-packing-plant processing of security checks finally complete all their small humiliations, your shoulders slowly unfurl from all the pent-up stress and you realize that for two days, for two weeks, a month, or maybe more, everything you know is thousands of miles away, and none of it can touch you. And it's at these times that alcohol, which has never, ever, done anyone any good, even at the best of times, becomes even more of a menace. Step away from the everyday and the consequences of drinking too much become conflated with the escape from responsibilities afforded by long-distance travel. So sure, yes, I will have another drink, why not, I'm not driving, I don't have to do a damn thing I don't want to, and it can't possibly affect me, because, after all, babe, I'm on vacation.

It generally goes something like this:

YVR. Arrive too early, at least two hours before I can even check in. I could get some books, maybe a decent newspaper or two, for a change. There's coffee, Starbucks of course, so it'll be bitter. Can't get into the duty-free, and I've seen The Spirit of Haida Gwaii before . . . hey, is that a bar over there?

—Pale Ale please . . .

—Pale Ale please . . .

—Pale Ale please . . .

—Sure, why not, another should be okay—can I smoke in here?

—Well, actually a scotch might be nice, I've still got a few minutes 'til check-in. Anyone ever tell you you look a lot like Barbra Streisand? Especially around the nose . . .

—Pale Ale, please . . . shorry about that Streisand comment—I really did mean it as a compliment, sheesh very talented . . .

—Yesh, just one carry-on . . . where? Ish right here . . . um . . . back in a minute.

—Waitressh . . . uh . . . Ms. Srieshand, did you shee ma bag?

And so on . . . until you're poured off the plane at the other end of the world, with a roiling stomach and a desperate head, and stern officials demand incomprehensible things from you in accents you can barely understand:

—You must pee first.

—Pardon?

—Pee. Then you can go in.

—Umm . . . but I went on the plane . . . a bunch of times.

—What?

—On the plane. I peed. Lots of times.

—No, pee here, not on plane. Pee first to get stamp.

—Oh, pay! Pay for the visa stamp. Ha! Do I pay you?

—No. Pee other line.

There you are with no wits about you when you need them most, and only yourself to blame, and yet in the back of your head you still think you've done the right thing because you've taken the only rational path and self-medicated to escape the nightmare at 35,000 feet that brought to you to this surreal crossroad in the first place.

In its soul-destroying arc between fear, boredom, and then more fear, flying mimics the psychological continuum of long-standing conflict, only you have the privilege of paying for the pain.

Travel truly is a type of time-stamped insanity. In fact, for someone who has never experienced it, the closest analogy I can think of to a bout of profound clinical depression is international air travel. In Economy Class. Somewhere around the fifth hour of an eight- or nine-hour trip, when the captain's just announced the plane's caught a headwind. Or just take the longest flight you've ever suffered through, then multiply it by a few months and you might begin to get an inkling of what's its like. You're anxious, trapped, with no ability to make any decision more important than chicken or beef, and the only really available direction is down. All the things you formerly enjoyed—food, books, movies, breathing—now spark nothing more than mild irritation, and every stretched minute brings you closer to the inevitable conclusion that you're never, ever, getting out of here alive.

So hold onto to those sleeping pills, miniature bottles, and inflatable headrests, all those small molecules of happiness that make it possible to get to the other end and out the door. Do whatever you can to get to foreign tarmac, strange air, and the manic hope of landing. It's worth it to find the world made anew, where every little thing is filled with interest, and possibility waits around every undiscovered corner. In the grace of arrival, every traveller has a moment as Adam or Eve; every destination, a freshly dewed garden.

▶

We're getting close to where we're going. There's been no announcement, but the time is about right, and all the seasoned travellers have already fled their seats for prime spots in the line-up outside the washrooms. I contemplate grabbing my carry-on from the overhead rack, to gain a few seconds when we disembark, but decide it's pointless: the flight's too full, and nobody's going anywhere anytime soon. Besides, the Scot's seat is starting to shake, and I think he's preparing for one last trip to the "secret place," and I hunker down in anticipation of another crossing. I wait as weird noises emanate from the window side, choked snuffles of amusement. I wonder if they're replaying *Shrek* again for some odd reason.

The Scot elbows my attention.

"Oh, look at this," he snuffles, a sideways smile cracking his face. "They're sly, those minxes. They've had one over on me." He waves the beer can at me. "This bloody thing is non-alcoholic."

The seatbelt light chimes, the captain comes on the air, and we wait for the world to rise to our expectations.

Allahua Akbar, Do You Read?

Inshallah. If Allah wills it. It's on the taxi-cabs in Mombasa, in Kenya. *Inshallah.* Both a profession of faith and a preparation for the inevitable, the proverb provides the cab drivers and their touts with the one guarantee their largely unregulated and regularly lethal profession demands: Immunity.

Mombasa is a small island, only fourteen square kilometers, and, with over seventy mosques, temples, and churches scattered around the city, it's hard to get away from God. Your fate is written on every street corner, not just the sides of converted Japanese mini-vans. From the stern injunction "Read Quran" arching over Digo Road, to the cries of "Come join us, brother" issuing from the huge blue-striped faith-healing tent on the other side of town, Mombasa is rife with overt exhortations to get a hold of some holy spirit.

And that's okay, no matter how deeply held your beliefs otherwise, because you know, almost as soon as you touch down at Moi International, that you're going to have to hold onto something and that you're going to need it now . . .

. . . off of Air Fear and into arrivals. Birds and cigarette butts at your feet. Unshaven Algerian diplomats at your shoulder. Exhaustion inside. Freed from the sterile familiarity of the airplane tube, you look around for the recognizable but meet only the lost looks of other tourists as your eyes and ears fill with the atmosphere of somewhere else. Following the locals—white Muslim caps and black bui-bui gowns—you wait at the world's slowest baggage carousel then light up with everybody else: No smoking signs are nonexistent here.

Finally, customs, and a grim altercation as the luggage of the South Asian couple in front of you is ripped apart by a flat-eyed customs official. The wife, veiled, fat and silent, stares at her feet as electrical items from their bags disappear behind the counter and her middle-aged husband repeats over and over with increasing desperation, "But I don't need a receipt for that, I tell you. I don't need a receipt." Pretty music plays over airport speakers: a Swahili song of welcome.

A quick change of line; a cursory passport glance: "Thank you. Asante. Enjoy your stay in Mombasa." And out. And it hits you as the heat claps down and you see the palm trees and your nose fills with the sweet smoke scent of Kenya and dark hands grab as cabbies mob you—"Taxi bwana? Finest on the island"—that, yes, you are in Africa, and, no, it's not what you expected.

I blame Marlin Perkins.
And his assistant, Jim. And Sally Struthers. Elspeth

Huxley and her flame trees. Beryl Markham. *Born Free.*
World Vision. The Happy Valley crowd. Isak Dinesen,
Denys Finch Hatton, and Baron Blixen. Live Aid. *The Lion
King.* We Are the World. *Out of Africa.* Almost every *National
Geographic* special ever made. All of those things that tell us
again and again that Africa can be boiled down to four
essentials: wild animals, starving children, tribal life, and gin
and tonics on the veranda.

Even the guide books get it wrong. Without exception
their descriptions of Mombasa centre around words like
"drowsy," "peaceful," "somnolent." All true enough in one
sense, the sense that you can never get anything done on
time, but none really convey even the casual visitor's impression of the city: an impression that would have to include
adjectives like "baffling," "demented," "desperate."

Although Mombasa's literally choked with cars, there are no
traffic lights in town. Or, at least, any that work. Regularly,
that is. One or two are up and running occasionally, but
never any longer than twenty-four hours — the length of time
it usually takes for someone to be surprised enough by the
sudden appearance of a shining stoplight to smash into its
supporting pole.

According to the local gossip columnist, "The Watchman,"
a government delegation went to the home of the city engineer in charge of traffic control to discuss the problem. When
they arrived, his wife told the delegation that the engineer
was out, but would be home shortly. That was four years

ago. All subsequent inquiries since have pretty much received the same response: The engineer is never in.

A strange situation, perhaps, but one that works out quite
well for almost everyone involved. Through their dogged pur-
suit of the absent engineer, city officials prove their zeal for
protecting the public good, and, by never actually spending
any public money on the traffic-light problem, demonstrate
their impeccable fiscal responsibility as well.

The engineer's well-timed disappearances also add to the
greater good, in the form of job security: as long as the traffic-
light system stays mostly out of order, he'll remain secure in
his position—there'll be no layoffs for one of the few recipients
of the maintenance training the Japanese provided along with
their stoplight project.

All in all, if everything stays the same, everybody does
okay.

Except for, of course, the other half-million or so
inhabitants of Mombasa: the people regularly mangled by late-
model vehicles run by drivers with no real experience of the
rules of the road. Traffic accidents are endemic in Kenya as
everybody drives with one hand on the horn and the other on
the afterlife. And the results of this handiwork can be seen
every day as the country's two national newspapers, *The Nation*
and *The Standard*, publish their running traffic-fatality totals.
Over two thousand the last time I looked. And that was only
halfway through the year.

Even in this gruesome context, driving in Mombasa
entails a special madness. It's not just the lack of stoplights,

street lamps, or centre lines that makes island driving especially dangerous. Or the city's "anything goes" attitude towards parking, potholes, and speed limits.

Nor is it all the ancient imports pushing their way through Old Town streets that were already too narrow to accommodate much more than a couple of Arab coffee sellers several hundred years ago.

It isn't the red amphetamine stem, *qat*, which all the truckers chew as they grind their load-shifted vehicles down crowded thoroughfares slick with stinking pools of water and rind. Or the thousands of migrant workers who stream onto the island and feed the Matatu drivers' frenzied struggle to grossly overload their taxi-vans as many times as possible in the shortest time available.

These aren't the things that make Mombasa driving dangerous.

What does make it dangerous is the idea that it all ends up with Allah; that if it's been willed, it's not your fault. With *Inshallah* comes a kind of extended coverage, an eliminated liability, which not only negates personal responsibility, but creates unlimited potential: the impossible drops its prefix when there's a good chance that it's the hand of God pushing you forward instead of your gas pedal. To the faithful, fitting a ten-foot car into a two-foot traffic gap is more a question of Will than physics. And if someone dies because of mere mathematics, well, it was their time. It would have happened anyway.

▶

I divided most of my time in Africa between Slaughter and War, the English translations of Tsavo and Mombasa respectively. Tsavo is one of the world's great parks — 20,000 square kilometres of things that would kill you given half the chance: thorny plants and poisonous insects, skittish carnivores and Cape buffalo, Somali poachers and AK-47s. The poachers gave the park's old Kikamba name a new relevance in the '70s and early '80s when they slaughtered about seventy percent of Tsavo's elephants and completely decimated the rhino population. Things have changed now though, with Kenya's implementation of a shoot-to-kill policy on poachers, and you can see elephants all over Tsavo East and West, usually small herds led by young females forced into dominance at too early an age. They are nervous and keep their distance from the safari cars touring the park.

Along with Amboseli and Masai Mara, Tsavo is one of the main stops on the great tourist migrations that sweep down to the Indian Ocean in the winter and summer months; down to the mainland coasts that hug Mombasa north and south. It is here where the city spreads off the island and into the high-end accommodation of hotel chains. The hotels themselves are luxurious affairs, like stationary cruise ships done in Swahili-style architecture with white stone walls and dark hardwood floors and rafters. Many are divided by nationality: the English stay at Nyali Beach, Germans at Diani, French at Sun and Sand. They like to keep their distance from one another.

Aside from quick package trips onto the island to shop for curios in Old Town and see the old Portuguese Fort that anchors one end of the city, the coast hotels are most tourists' main experience of Mombasa. And they get exactly what they pay for—sun-drenched days in a tropical paradise full of food, drink, waiters, and floor shows. Peace of mind at $120 a day.

"Jambo, rafiki, my name is Omar. You are English, yes?"

The beaches on the coast are stunning. White sand and palm trees shouldering calm green reef waters for miles and miles. Postcard perfect, and almost completely deserted.

"Hakuna matata? Yes, that is Swahili—no problems, just like me, Omar . . . What is Lion King?"

All the hotels have two or more pools and all the pools face the beach, separated from the sand by grass and low retaining walls that give unobstructed views of the Indian Ocean. Generally, tourists stay on the pool side of the stone wall, leaving Africa on the other. Six inches, two solitudes.

"You are going to the reef? You will need a guide, and I can show you the safest way."

The reason why most tourists don't complete their Club Med fantasies and spend ages strolling barefoot down those endless miles of pristine beach bobs up over the wall every few minutes. It is the dark head of a young man. And each time he pops above the stone crest of the retaining wall, he brings up his hand in a jerky thumbs-up motion as if invisible strings are pulling him to the sky. Up and down he goes, trying to catch indifferent eyes hidden under black glasses, until a guard finally chases him off and he is replaced by another of the dozens of beach boys that seem to materialize any time a Westerner sets foot on the sand, all of them wanting to shake your hand, say their name, and sell you something: carvings, key chains, their "sisters," themselves.

"Wait! Wait! Looking is free. You can look for free. Hakuna matata. Hakuna matata!"

Of course, everybody tries to stroll and suntan on the beaches at first. But there are just too many beach boys, and they're just too persistent, for anybody to stay on the sand for too long. Eventually even the most stubborn tourist retreats back into his hotel to sit by the pool and watch the bobbing heads and rolling waves just down there at the end of the enclave and at the edge of Africa. And as you sit there and you sip your beer and watch the world move up and down and in and out, everything beyond that wall seems to slip; to become separate and surreal. Detached. Immune. And all of a sudden all that bad driving makes sense.

"Jambo, rafiki, my name is Omar . . . ."

▶

There is a naked woman standing on the centre divider in the middle of Kilindi road in the heart of the city. She is silent and stares at the passing cars as she runs one hand after the other through the dirty tangle of her wiry hair. Her heavy breasts move in rhythm with her arms in a dark, fleshy dance. She is mad, says my driver, Ali. There are many crazy people here.

Ali and I are running errands and we're running late. Not that either of us really care—we enjoy each other's company. Or, rather, I quite like Ali. Personally, I suspect he thinks I'm an idiot because he sniggers at almost everything I say, something that makes absolute sense since I spend most of my time with him spouting demands for barbecued goat and bigger beer in kitchen Swahili:

Nyama choma. Heh-heh.

Nataka Tusker kubwa. Heh-heh.

Sasa hivi. Heh-heh.

A black and white Beavis and Butthead.

I do know, though, that Ali is happy to take me on these daily tours around town since I buy him *qat* almost every time we go. For about a dollar you can buy a bundle the size of your head and we mix it with Big-G bubble gum and chew on huge pink wads of the stuff as we tool around the island in our ancient red Toyota. Ali loves *qat*, but I find the taste too bitter and the effect too mild. All it does speed up my speech and make my lips go numb as the stem-laced gum flops around my mouth like an extra tongue and I spastically punch the radio in search of extra channels, even though I know it doesn't work.

Ali, what is the frequency? Heh-heh.

So there we are, a couple of tardy *qat*-heads sniggering and fidgeting and moving too fast in an aimless search for mangoes and cheese, and we're floating on the traffic stream, a blur of colour and light and movement, and I love it. Three months of constant travel has turned me into a kind of ground shark and I will get on anything that is going anywhere: I don't even wear a seat belt anymore. Constant motion is all that matters and Mombasa gives it to me. It makes me feel like I'm inside a Tide commercial: everything is in-your-face, brighter than bright and louder than it should be. And as I flash by all the bright white buildings with rotten tops like stained crowns on badly capped teeth, past all the eye-stretching ads for Omo cleaning detergent, Peptang tomato sauce, Rooster and Embassy cigarettes, the neon-reds, the neon-yellows and blues of all the cars and clothes blend with the blare of horn and Matatu music and the whole thing becomes a kind of living Pollock action painting, and I feel freer than I have ever felt before . . . until the cripple tries to cross the road.

I had seen this beggar before — Mombasa is small enough to get to know most of them by sight, if not by name — but almost always on the sidewalk. His paralyzed legs stick out straight in front of him and he walks on his hands like a gymnast riding a pommel horse. Now he was on the road, snaking and shoulder-rolling his way through the rushing traffic on a dangerous journey to the other side. And, somehow, he's made it, but he's also made a miscalculation because the sidewalk is broken and slabs of it are blocking his way to safety. He's scrabbling and flopping against the upturned cement like a shell-less turtle right in front of Ali and me, and I know we can't stop in time and at that moment everything slows and I see a little further and jump the life to come . . .

. . . A hollow thud, and the car bucks and clutches like a row of teeth scudding down a cob of corn until it finally, finally stops. Everything outside is quiet. All I can hear is Ali's hissing breath beside me, but the sound grows faint as the buzz of hornets gradually fills my head. My hand is on the door handle, but I can't open it; I can't take that responsibility, even though I have to. I don't look at Ali, even though I want to, instead I look Out There, through the windshield, and I see people, stopped, standing in a half-circle. I see faces still and staring. And under the pressure of their eyes, my hand moves, the door opens and I see blood oozing its way down the incline of the potted road. Its colour is dull and flat and, as I look, the hornets leave my head, I hear a cry, and the crowd moves towards me . . .

Blood—blood on my knuckle. I've cut my hand on a chunk of seat metal in a last-ditch effort to grab my belt and strap myself away from the inevitable. I swear and clutch the dashboard and look up to see the beggar die, but the space where he was is simply road and broken sidewalk and we're still rolling on the traffic stream, heading off somewhere else in a roar of colour and light. I unclench my teeth and crane my neck trying to see what could've possibly happened, but we're already too far past to see that far back, and Ali is snickering and looking at me as if I'm crazy as I demand, again and again, to know what happened to that man.

"What beggar?" says Ali. "What man?"

Heh-heh.

▶

Outside of Nyali Bridge, one of the main gateways onto the island, is Kisauni village. At first glance this little mud-and-wattle town looks desperately poor and horribly depressing, but after a while, and a few closer looks, it becomes clear that it's actually a pretty decent, hard-working place. In fact, if anyone decided to spend even a little time there, they could learn at least a half a dozen trades that would earn a very decent income anywhere in the West. Unfortunately, it doesn't work that way in Kisauni, and most people there can't even afford electricity, no matter how hard they work.

Because very few people have power in Kisauni, almost everyone uses candles or storm lanterns for light after dark. And when you drive through the centre of Kisauni after the sun has gone down, it looks like the entire village has been replaced with a huge bowl-shaped mirror reflecting distant suns as thousands of tiny flickering lights surround you in every direction. And if you pass through the village at just the right time, you can hear the Call, the Adhan, coming from all those mosques all over the island. At first, a single wailing cry calling the faithful to come and pray. *Ahhaalla-hoaa Ahhkbarrrr.* And then another, and another as the call is caught in one throat, held, shaped and strengthened, then passed to the next, and the next, and the next, until the whole island echoes with Allah and the stars fill your eyes and you float through the sky with the sound of God inside.

Forty-foot Love

The boy plunges into the water, brine filling nose and ears, the cold first numbing his head, then clearing it as his body registers the cruel shock of an alien terrain. Clockwork strokes and summer-stained arms drive him deeper, towards chillier depths and the blurry dapple of rock, sand, and waving seaweed. Through the burgeoning pressure in his ears he can hear the insistent crackle of hungry sea-life and the hum of distant motorboats.

Fingers brush bottom and he grabs a handful of sand — the ritual end of another summer morning.

A quick kick and he rises, arms outstretched, fingers loosing a spreading stream of silt. He turns in a slow corkscrew, surrendering to the pull of the sun and the mammalian demand for oxygen and surface. He breaks through, sucking air in quiet gasps, lungs still tight from the cold. Water courses into his eyes and he strains through sting and salty chop to see what he just left: endless blue, and a deserted tree-ringed bay dotted by wharves and anchored sailboats. Glimpses of civilization up on the bank: his home peeking out from behind breeze-blown branches.

Pulling himself past hairy strands of clotted mussels and

worm-eaten wood, the boy heaves up onto the dock, its creosote smell filling his nostrils. He shivers in the heat, salt-water trickling from slicked hair, drips falling from nose to thin chest, as he slides onto his towel and presses his back onto the cool hull of the upturned dinghy behind him. He edges his toes over the side, squinting at the shimmer of the empty bay, waiting to warm as the wind licks the salt from his body and the dock rocks him into the quick amnesiac slumber of an eternal summer day.

▶

Up in the balcony, I shudder against the air-conditioned stream buffeting the back of my neck. Clutching my cooling coffee close, I try to burrow down into the low unyielding back of the hard seat as I survey the surrounding chairs for somewhere — anywhere — warmer. But the four-hundred-odd seats of the Directors Guild Theatre were already mostly full at this ungodly hour, testament to the lecturer's fierce reputation. I was sure that shades of Brian Cox's bullying performance in Adaptation had flickered through everyone's head at least once that morning; nobody had dared to push the snooze button on their alarm clocks today. No one wanted to start their day as a tardy and cowering Nicolas Cage.

The quiet chimes of starting laptops whisper throughout the theatre, tinny counterpoints to the low mutter of early-morning introductions. Soft glows light seatbacks—21st century fireplaces. Out of oversized bags come notepads and pens, highlighters, and the crinkle of diminutive snacks. Everywhere, copies of the bible—*Story*: the collected wisdom of the wizard about to materialize before us.

My eyes settle in the lap of the young woman beside me, envying the thick woolen cover on her lap.

"That was smart," I said, catching her attention. "Bringing a blanket. I never would have thought about it, especially with weather being this good. Who expects New York to be so hot in October? It's a real . . ."

Unfamiliarity with my seatmate, and the slight tinge of her skin, kicks in the polite pressure of political correctness. Indian summer stops at tongue tip.

"My name's Jim, by the way."

"Evelyn." The quick welcoming press of a cool hand.

"So you're from around here?"

Here. Manhattan, and the roar of the billion-footed beast. Concrete canyons alive with endless traffic and the thrum of pressured hearts.

"Close. Brooklyn, about ten minutes away by train."

"I . . . we're . . . from Canada . . . Vancouver." I gesture to the woman on my left. "This is Gaye, my writing partner."

Gaye cranes her head out of the nest she's made from our jackets and smiles a weary hello.

"Vancouver—I hear it's pretty there. Lots of mountains."

"Yeah, it's pretty," says Gaye, "if you like mountains."

Drained by this small outburst of muted enthusiasm, Gaye retreats back into her Gore-Tex nest, her usual conversational torrent choked by chill and jet lag.

"It's way more expensive here though," I add, filling up the brief silence with a boost for my hometown. "Bought a salad last night. Cost me eighteen bucks."

Evelyn snorts. "Midtown. Forget about it. Nobody buys their food here." She reaches into a nearby knapsack, pulls out a clear plastic bag stuffed with sandwiches. "Student budget."

We talk briefly about our respective university lives. Mine, finished a few years back after far too long a stay. Appalling GPA. Evelyn, a bit more successful. Masters' student in the creative writing program at NYU. Stuck halfway through a collection of short stories. Decided to roll the dice and spend most of her savings on this seminar.

"I blew my food budget for the next month on this," she says. "This'll either be the best or worst thing I ever did."

"I guess you've got about thirty hours to figure that one out—apparently we all do,"

I say.

A groan from Gaye at the reminder of the marathon lecture we'll be sitting through for the next three days, followed by a cavernous yawn. I stifle the urge to do the same, coffee losing the fight with fatigue.

Almost no sleep for either of us last night. Late arrival, panic at the airport. Can't find the car service we'd carefully prearranged in Vancouver. Dash around LaGuardia, trying different exits and transit stands, placing frantic phone calls from grubby pay phones to an exasperated dispatcher — "Your car is there. Your driver is circling the airport. They're not allowed to park more than a minute, you know. It's the law. You have to meet him outside arrivals."

Finally someone points us in the right direction — we'd been on the wrong level all this time — and we stumble into the calm interior of our Town Car with quick apologies and the heartfelt promises of a big tip.

Off into the night and New York City. Low brownstones and weathered neighbourhood stores slip past darkened windows. The traffic is fairly light at the moment, but for no apparent reason our driver changes lanes every few minutes, constantly pattering about his recent driving record as he slides across broken lines, all the while making a disconcerting amount of eye contact — "Four accidents already this year. People just don't signal in this town."

I watch him switch lanes again. His fingers never stray from the steering wheel. Eyes barely leave ours. It's true. No one signals here.

Over the bridge and into Manhattan proper. The island itself is flat — completely levelled in some Grand Plan cooked up a couple of hundred years ago, but it feels as if we've descended into some odd and angular valley as elegant skyscrapers and stacks of apartment buildings stuffed with air conditioners block out the night sky. A stream of yellow cabs flood the streets around us, all of them seemingly filled with well-dressed passengers out for a night on the only town that ever mattered. Their expensive attire makes me abruptly conscious of my own ratty sneakers and worn green corduroys. I don't have the right clothes for this city, and I feel like I've arrived at the wrong party. Out of place and shrinking in consequence as everything around me scales upwards.

We scoot past Central Park. Dodge the postcard cliché of a horse-drawn carriage. On the street: everyone. I've never seen so many people. It's 12:15 at night.

"Okay we're here," says our driver, miraculously finding a spot right in front of our hotel's yellow awning.

Crowds push past our car, parting only for the stocky pillars of doormen planted securely on the sidewalk. Everything is oddly lit, dimly pulsing in the huge neon cloud emanating from a few blocks away.

Gaye and I hesitate, both abruptly afraid to step out and leave the familiar comfort of the Town Car security zone.

"You're sure this is it? Maybe there's another Wellington somewhere else. It didn't look this close to Times Square on the map."

"This is it," says the driver, his patient face reflecting "out-of-towner." "Don't forget your bags."

Gaye pushes a bunch of bills at him—far too large a tip—and we're out. A gust of warm night air and a slight garbage smell from thigh-high piles of bagged refuse awaiting pick-up. We quickstep through the sidewalk throng and into an equally crowded lobby: a pack of German tourists crowd the check-in as a flushed trio of Puerto Rican clerks try to punch through language barriers and hand out keycards as quickly as possible.

Twenty minutes later and we're dropping bags in our room. It's small, dingy, with two single beds, a dirty carpet, and cracked bathroom tiles. Its only window looks out onto a light well and a looming brick wall. A steal at $285 dollars a night.

"At least we won't be spending too much time in here," I say.

Three flights down an ill-lit stairwell, the elevator far too overburdened by paunchy German tourists to be of any possible use. Past the still-crowded reception desk — freshly arrived Australians milling about it now — and the in-house barbershop proudly displaying pictures of David Letterman grimacing a gap-toothed smile in one of its old-fashioned chairs. Through the doors, down the avenue, and into the heart of Times Square.

In the centre of the city, a commercial supernova. Everywhere, the greedy pulse of storeys-high neon and a mind-melting roll of LED animations, their millions of multi-coloured bulbs screaming "buy" at the unbelievably crowded sidewalks below. The fabled grit of years-gone-by replaced by a kind of garish game reserve for multinationals. No panhandlers, pushers, or Midnight Cowboys in sight. Instead, unfettered avarice reaching JumboTron proportions on $300,000-a-month displays. All of the Square's fabled darkness banished by billboards beaming the dubious delights of Coca-Cola and M&M's, Toys "R" Us and the endless scroll of Wall Street's end-of-day results.

My eyes sweep past McDonald's ubiquitous golden arches and the gaudy enticement of Hershey's saccharine spectacular —215 feet of Kisses and Twizzlers and York Peppermint Patties—then slide over acres of ads for Applebees, Virgin Records, *Lion King,* and *Les Mis.* I look down Broadway and upwards, ingesting the gargantuan Budweiser sign and billowing steam of the Nissin noodle cup perpetually cooling on the side of One Times Square.

Gaye snaps a picture, her flash an impotent flicker against the towering Kodak sign beating down on us.

"You hungry?" I say.

We duck into a packed deli, grab bowls of take-out salad—eighteen dollars each—sprint back to our room for a fast bite and an attempt at much-needed unconsciousness. But both of us are too exhilarated by our bite of the city to sleep. All we achieve are brief respites under scratchy blankets; fitful snoozes broken by the clank of the air exchanger just under our window and the sound of scurrying under our beds: likely something feasting on dropped leaves of overpriced salad. Neither of us willing to look underneath and spoil the gift of a great location.

The phone rings. Our 6:30 a.m. wake-up call. A quick wash, a change into clothes from the night before, and out.

Into brilliant day. We charge onto 7th Avenue and—caught

in a herd of blue-shirted businessmen yelling at each other through headsets—head the wrong way for a few blurred blocks. Regaining our bearings, we reverse direction, dash into a crammed deli just up the avenue, and grab bagged coffee and bagels to go. Mouths crammed with cream cheese we charge on, already sweating in the sunshine, iconic landmarks occasionally poking into surprised consciousness—"Hey, look, Carnegie Hall."

West 57th. Turn right. Walk a block. Then part of another. There it is. Duck through the entrance and grab our ID badges, then up and into theatre seats. We sit, waiting with Evelyn in icy anticipation while—just outside those doors— big city and sunshine whisper warm escape.

I touch Gaye's shoulder. "You okay?"

"I'm freezing, I'm tired. I hate this already."

A smattering of applause and I look at the stage. The claps grow louder, stronger, as they ripple through the crowd. People rising as a bushy-browed figure strides onto the stage. Smiling slightly, the man lets the applause wash over him briefly, gestures for quiet, stands centre stage. Robert McKee is ready. The story of story about to begin.

▶

They would be here soon. Day-trippers from mega-mall suburbs. Hot-dogging water-skiers eager to try out trick skis and back flips on the ramp across the bay. Sleek party yachts anchoring together in the flats for wine- and scandal-soaked weekends. Soon, there'd be laughter, music, and indiscreet conversation skipping across the water's surprisingly capable acoustics, and the rocky beaches would ring with the elated shrieks of local kids finally freed from the dry confines of day care.

But for now the bay was his.

And it was his. All of it. He'd spent seventeen years exploring its shores, shallows, and depths. Watching its mood from his kitchen window every morning. The lap of its waters an ever-present lull in his daily life. Every wave and trough a dip into his personal history.

There at the sandy patch beside the big boulder, that was where he'd learned to swim. Roughhousing with friends in the shallows: a push, then over his head. Desperate dog-paddling until his feet clawed bottom. His friends laughing, splashing: oblivious to the watery gurgle of the life and death struggle just behind them.

There at the boathouse just along the shore, warm nights of Spin the Bottle, Truth or Dare, and the tentative slide of hands under wet bathing suits. Up there on those cliffs leading up to Indian Arm, ancient pictographs, faded reminders of long-gone inhabitants, hidden behind scraggly pines.

Nearby, wrecks. He'd watched visiting divers, so he knew their location. Sub-chasers and mine-sweepers, WWII salvage—sunk for safety's sake. The bay's bright chop betrayed nothing of the dead killing machines decaying a hundred feet below.

The best fishing: near the generating station. That dead tree: an eagle perch. In that embankment, a shallow cave created by the half-roll of a huge granite stone, a place to hide childhood marbles and the illicit bottles of teenage years.

A swell hit the docks, sending spray over the boy's feet. He roused briefly, glanced out at the bay. Eyes wandered over water, past where the ski-boat had sunk last summer, just beyond it to the spot where the Randalls' marriage had ended.

The Randalls moved into the Walshes' old house, and fit in quickly with the well-established rhythms of the village. Helping out with annual fishing derbies, Christmas pageants, and Easter-egg hunts. Opening their house to parents with free time, the Randalls artfully steered their two children into friendships with neighbourhood kids.

She — Mrs. Randall — was forty-ish, fading, making up for time's blear slide with a little extra make-up and a slightly forced vivaciousness. Holding it all together, still pretty and trim, but not quite able to dam the trickle of need leaking from her edges.

"Hi, Mrs. Randall. Is Francis here?"

We'd come to collect her son for some ill-considered adventure, timing it so she'd be sun tanning in her usual perch on the patio. There she was: bikini-clad, lounging in a green lawn chair, a wine glass in her hands. Spying us, she stood and half-turned away, her face towards us over tanned shoulder: "Am I done yet?"

She laughed, and pulled at the bottom of her suit, showing

a bit of cheek so we could see the tan divide and the taboo swell of forbidden skin.

"Francis is in his room. C'mon over and say hello before you get him."

Then kisses on the lips — held just that second too long — followed by the embarrassed shuffles of teenage boys looking past the mom and at the lithe woman hinting promise.

When Francis emerged from the house, none of us could look him in the eye.

He — Mr. Randall — possessed a great charm, the bonhomie of the good neighbour with the well-stocked tool shed and an ever-burning barbecue. Always ready with a joke and a tall tale, yet all told with a slight distance in his eyes: a wary gulf that confirmed his kids' stories of strictness and a swift and terrible temper. A strong man, but sadly obese, wattles of fat overwhelming the fit and handsome self Mrs. Randall married many years before.

Over the summer they'd made friends with the yacht crowd that anchored near the flats on the weekend. Shouted pleasantries from the Randall's close-by dock had led to an open-ended invitation, and on select sunny days a skiff would be sent to collect them.

On board, khaki shorts, well-padded bellies, deep tans, and deck shoes. Thin summer dresses slipped over tiny bikinis. Loud music, an open bar, more what-the-hell attitude as the weekend wore on. Topless sunbathing and drunken dives from top decks. Elegant dinners at sunset. Dancing, late into the night.

Mr. Randall stumbled out onto a deserted section of the yacht's deck; stars slightly smudged by the double vision of two many mojitos. He reached under a layer of untucked shirt and into a deep pocket in his loose-fitting pants. Fished out a lighter and a long-forbidden cigarette. Lighting it, he drew deeply and leaned against what looked like firm rail. The unsecured gate smacked open; 275 pounds dropped thirty feet: a shocked belly-flop into cold black water.

Arm badly strained by the plummet, by the concrete force of flat water meeting uncontrolled fall, Mr. Randall clawed his way to the surface and looked up at a sheer curve of white wall. No ropes or ladders apparent, the low skiff usually tied to the yacht out on a cocktail call at another vessel.

He worked his way along the sides of the boat in limping paddles, bellowing for help, drowned out by the shriek of laughter, drums, and electric guitar. Fluorescent bubbles swirled around his clumsy strokes, orbs buoyed by moonlight.

There. A face. Looking over the railing. His wife. "Angie, for god's sake get help."

He waited. She watched, her eyes black holes in the night. And he realized, as she wordlessly turned back to the party—to the sweet call of young men and real champagne— that no help was ever arriving.

Thirty minutes later he lay half sunk on hard shore, shivering in a slick gruel of seawater vomit. Completely certain of new life and distant seas—salmon fishing in Alaska.

Yes, they would be here soon, thought the boy. The sun's position promised an imminent arrival, but for now the bay belonged to him, and he stood and dived off the dock, letting its cool waters slide through his embrace.

▸

We will not be late.

We will not interrupt. No uninvited questions or opinions. None.

We will not dare hand him scenes, stories, or scripts expecting help or informal critique. Ever.

And we will definitely not "have conversations on your fucking cell phones while I am talking."

McKee pauses, smiles. "As you may have noticed I like to fucking swear."

Writers generally make poor public speakers. Their calling is tailor-made for social isolates whose best lines flow from the considered touch of fingertip and the safe distance of the printed page. For them, a public reading, and the actual possibility of facing a crowd of living human beings, is a tightrope shuffle between controlled panic and whiskey courage.

Not McKee. No nervous coughs, trembling hands, or hesitations for him. No eye-rolling searches for absent words or awkward glances at ill-lit notes hastily scrawled on yellow pad. The sixty-four-year-old strides around the stage empty handed and supremely confident in his subject matter. He's at home, enjoying himself, an actor in his element, a quarter-century of practiced craft peeking behind every well-timed pause and the fierce delivery of his torrential address. Make no doubt about it, Robert McKee is religiously devoted to the well-told story and this thirty-six-hour sermon is his passion play. We—the audience—more spectators than students, only allowed to witness his fervor on his terms, at his sufferance. And we're happy to sacrifice hard-earned pieces of silver to be there in person.

After all, McKee's *Story* seminar is legendary. A lifetime of ardent learning about the substance of story dispensed over three marathon days. The lectures themselves take place at major cities all over the world—he's off to Tel Aviv after this New York seminar and then London after that—and he's been following a similar schedule for well over twenty years. Attendees at the seminars range from neophyte scribblers to a who's-who of established novelists, actors, and screenwriters. Lots of Academy Award winners. Peter Jackson and Quentin Tarantino have both been attendees. Other bright lights, and the list is very, very long, include David Bowie, Kirk Douglas, and Gloria Steinem. John Cleese has been in this audience as well, three times at last count. McKee's book *Story* is in its twentieth U.S. printing. The most overused description of him is "guru."

We're only about an hour and a half into the art of story, and my hand is already starting to cramp from all the pressured scrawls I'm making on my yellow pad. I want to make certain that I let nothing escape.

The pain's fitting though, as McKee's already made it pretty evident that by writing we're already following an exceedingly hard road full of suffering. He's also made it abundantly clear that most of us will crash and burn on the trip. But he is encouraging, treating us as peers for the time being, pointing out the opportunities that lie in the huge demand for a good story and the equal lack of reliable supply. Hollywood alone puts in over half a billion dollars per year in its attempt to get material decent enough to put onto celluloid. Most of that money goes into work that never gets made. All this talk of plentiful cash makes me drift into a short greedy haze, and I idly wonder how much McKee rakes in a year from his book and seminars. More than I'll ever see, that's for sure.

I also wonder if his attire is representative of how the wealthy dress these days. His pants and shoes are brand new, presumably purchased for this performance. They look like off-brands and the jeans are so stiff they almost make his legs redundant; his sneakers so white I'm transfixed by their paces.

I pull myself out of the white light of his footwear and into the decline of story. McKee's outlining a general failure throughout the arts to learn and properly apply principle and craft, then delves into storytellers' current propensity to apply received wisdom to their work rather than real experience tempered by self-knowledge. It's a corrupting reliance, one that extends to language, to the very words used to tell a tale. You can see it in the discourse of political correctness, for example, and how its mewling terminology reflects eroded meaning, values, and, most importantly, truths.

"People are not differently abled," roars McKee. "They are handicapped. They are cripples."

A few nervous laughs as everyone avoids looking at the lone wheelchair perched at the top of one of the aisles.

Gaye snorts, taps my hand and shuffles to a highlighted line in her copy of his book. "Story is about respect, not disdain, for the audience," it reads.

▶

The slide of feet and flip-flops down the steep embankment, pebbles dropping over rough-hewn steps.

It's her.

The boy sits up quickly, shrugs on his short-sleeved shirt, suddenly conscious of his underdeveloped chest. He buttons it partway, covering just enough to feel comfortable, and then lies back, looking downward in cool eye-slit repose.

The ramp shudders with sudden weight, its derelict springs squealing rusty complaint. Then the wooden echo of quick steps just above the waterline.

He'd met Luanne about a month ago, both of them falling into the same lazy orbit around the dock when their summer vacations coincided. She was a few years older than he, just moving into her twenties. Worked as a part-time reception-ist at a body shop. Filled the rest of her days with devoted tanning and nursing courses. She lived in a half-duplex three houses down that belonged to the same local land baron who owned the house his own family had rented for close to two decades. Moved in about six months ago with two mostly absent roommates. Loved travel and long-distance swims. Had a cat: a mutant white Persian with six toes on each foot. Blonde sun-bleached hair. No boyfriend.

Footsteps beside him now, followed by the quiet snicker of eased-off shoes. Through half-closed lashes he sees painted toes and deeply tanned feet. A waft of coconut as her towel is opened and spread. The warm tingle of skin propped close by.

"You know, some people are working right now," he says, eyes still stuck on splintered deck.

He turns at look to at her as she lifts shades and laughs, green eyes glinting in sunlight.

"Yeah, I've heard some people do that," she replies.

Their fingers brush each other across terrycloth and she leaves her hand where it lies. In her unhurried touch, vague hope and the murmured promise of bright days to come.

▶

"Character is revealed by pressure, by choices made when facing conflict. And the conflict…"

A belch from McKee. He holds his chest, looks stricken at his body's impolite interruption: "Excuse me."

"Foie gras," I whisper to Gaye.

It's the third day, twenty-ninth hour, and we're just back from lunch. In our case, tasteless sandwiches in Central

Park, in McKee's, something a little more refined. Just before the break, he'd explained where to get the best goose liver in New York, his disdain for political correctness apparently extending to food. Now it sounds as if the pâté is punching back.

He burps again. Another heartfelt apology.

I don't know about the others in the audience, but I'm actually fine with these gassy disruptions, relieved to see McKee having a human moment at last. The man's been a lecture machine over the last three days. A torrent of talk about story structure unbroken by film clips or other visual aids except for the occasional overhead and simply drawn diagram. So far we've covered classical design, Aristolean drama, turning points, inciting incidents, and the negative of the negative. We've learned how beats build to scenes, scenes lead to sequences, and how everything culminates in irreversible change. We've dipped into genre and *Die Hard*, writer's block and research, *Diabolique* and image systems inspired by drowning. Scene design, act design, principles of antagonism and exposition: we've delved into them too, plus the overarching importance of the controlling idea and authentic characters. Throughout it all, fervid reminders to take our art seriously, to avoid cheap tricks and, above all, tell the truth:

"M. Night Shyamalan got a ten-million-dollar deal because of *The Sixth Sense*. He doesn't deserve it. I guarantee you the rest of his movies will be bad. They will be flops. The man does not know how to tell an honest story."

Not too much more to go now, according to the schedule. Looks like we'll be into character and creative process for a bit, then we'll finally watch a film: a six-hour scene-by-scene analysis of *Casablanca*.

A light touch on my knee. I turn my attention from the stage.

"I can't," says Gaye. "I'm sorry, but I can't."

"Pardon? Can't what?"

"Stay here any longer. This is great, really great, but I need to get out."

"You can't leave. We're almost done. Besides you'd shoot me if I abandoned you."

She smiles. "True, but you don't know what you're missing. I do."

"What's that supposed to mean?"

"It means I've been to New York before."

She leans closer, her conspiratorial whisper clear above McKee's erudite rumble. "Wanna come with me?"

With the question comes a deep pang, the pulled blade of openly uttered desire. Flashes of Woody Allen's black-and-white love poem float through my head, quickly stalked by the steamy grime of Scorsese's mean streets. The writers might be in here, I think, but all the stories are out there.

I lift my almost-full yellow pad, the fourth I've filled so far. "Who's going to take notes?"

"It's all in the book, remember? He told us we didn't really need to take notes if we just wanted to listen."

It's true. I've even seen people in the audience dragging

their fingers along printed lines as McKee lectures. I've just blocked it out. Too proud of my notes to reject cognitive dissonance and accept all the wasted effort.

"So, coming or not? I figure we can get in about nine hours of sightseeing before we have to take off for the airport." She pauses, her hand grasping my forearm for emphasis. "I love this town, and there's no way I'm going to miss it."

Beyond those doors, Brooklyn Bridge and the Empire State. Grand Central Station, Greenwich Village, and the empty devastation of Ground Zero. Wall Street, Broadway, Rockefeller Center, Central Park, Harlem . . . Gaye zips her jacket, waits for a response.

"Dialogue is not conversation," yells McKee down below.

"Please, don't leave me here," I say.

▸

A low mosquito whine, growing louder as it approaches.

"So I see our friends are coming," says Luanne.

He knew who she was talking about without opening his eyes. He'd heard enough ski-boats to recognize their different drones. A Bayliner. Brent and his crew. The boy had been down here the first day they'd arrived, when they'd stumbled onto the bay after a twenty-minute ride from a public launch just up the inlet. They'd needed a place to ski from and the neglected dock, so different from all the other tidy wharves with their "No Trespassing" signs on prominent display, looked like it'd do. They'd pulled up, assumed his parents owned the beaten wharf, offered cold beer, asked permission to stay. He'd collected undeserved rent ever since: canned Kokanee, quick skis, dirty jokes, and rough company.

"You're surprised? They're here almost every day," the boy replied.

"Not usually this early. I try to avoid them. The last time I was down here when they were around I saw one of them peeing off the end of the dock, just hanging it out as if no one was here at all."

The boy looks at her, laughs. "Yeah, they're definitely not shy."

Luanne's nose crinkles in disgust. "They're animals. Pigs," she says.

"No, dogs," offers the boy with a snigger. "Junkyard dogs."

The whine swells to a snarl, cut back quickly as the ski-boat is pushed into neutral. The Bayliner rides its own wake up to the wharf, arriving with the acrid gurgle of idling engine and the smell of low-grade petrol. Wash rocks the dock, riding up on the deck, slightly wetting terrycloth towel as music blares — Top-40 AM radio. Four people onboard: Brent; the owner, two of his revolving ski-buddy crew, and a heavy brunette in an orange tube top.

Brent props himself higher in his seat, bare shoulders and chest muscles flexing over steering wheel as he cranes for a better vantage point at the fast-approaching dock. One of his buddies throws bumpers over the side, getting them out just before the boat rubs hard against barnacled wood.

Brent snaps off the engine, jumps out with beer can and bowline in hand.

"You're always here," Brent says to the boy. "Don't you ever go home?"

"We are home," replies Luanne.

Brent casts an appraising look, his eyes obvious as they sweep over browned body.

Luanne meets his stare with lifted shades. "You got our towels wet."

He turns and ties up the boat. The rest of the crew tosses skis and coolers on deck.

Brent reaches into a cooler. "You guys wanna beer?"

The boy nods practiced agreement, cracks the tossed can with thanks. Luanne reaches into her bag, waves a California Cooler.

"No thanks," she says. "I don't drink domestic. All those preservatives."

The crew gets their gear ready. One puts on a wetsuit and half-plunges in, his hands clutching the dock, holding his shaggy head above water. He curses the cold, and hurriedly pulls himself up. Dips gleaming skis in the water, wetting their rubber bindings for easier access. The brunette coils ski-rope in the cockpit. She's bent over and the bottom curve of her white ass peers out from the damp stringy edges of sea-worn cut-offs.

Brent glugs his beer, drops the can into the pile of unused lifejackets on the bottom of the boat.

"Gotta take care of some business," he says. "Then we'll head out for a ski."

He heads up the ramp and then steps off the wooded trail leading to the dock. Just barely behind some bushes, he shrugs himself into position. The torrent can be heard clearly down below.

Eye rolls from Luanne. A shake and huge belch from above.

Brent stomps back down the dock and pops himself on the Bayliner's bow, bare feet pushing its side off the dock as the boat rides slow swells. Behind, his wet-suited friend sits on wharf's edge, his skis in the water, bright red tips tilted just out of the sea. The brunette hands him the rope handle and the other man takes the shotgun position, facing stern and ready to spot.

Luanne slides herself on top of the upturned dinghy. Eye level and opposite Brent.

"Hey, you know kids play in that bush. They've got a little fort in there." Voice cool. Words enunciated, clear, challenging. "If you lived here you'd know that," she adds.

Brent smirks at his pals. "I guess they got a little moat to go with their fort now," he says.

Harsh laughter. The boy joins in, then chokes down his amusement, giggles stifled by the quick flit of betrayal across Luanne's face.

She waits for the others to stop. Tries again. "You should go before you come here. This isn't a public toilet."

Brent squints at her, eyes hard in the harsh glare. "You nuts? Go where?"

"Not here. It's private property." No change in Luanne's voice, but her toes clench the towel.

Brent points a thumb at the boy. "He said it was all right."

He's hit by the curt deposit of complete and undivided attention. Luanne's brows lift slightly in their wait for a united front. Scowls and flat anticipation from the others.

"Well, technically, it's not our dock," he says, voice tight, scaling higher. "It's in front of my house but we . . . I . . . don't own it. We rent . . . just like Luanne here."

The boy looks at her face, sun-kissed, stony . . . beautiful.

Brent tips his head back under the weight of a snide half-smile. "So, *technically*," he says, the word drawn out by sarcasm's deliberate stretch, "we have just as much right to be here as you do."

"*Technically*," he adds, looking straight at Luanne, "you guys can fuck right off."

No one says anything more, but, as the skiers take off for a quick slalom, then circle round and soak them with territorial spray, and Luanne slides into the water, turns on her back, and slices out towards faraway waves, the boy knows all he can do is stand up, dry off, and go away.

►

Gaye's gone — off to roam around her city about seven hours ago. Ilsa's left too, taken away by mist, heartbreak, and airplane. Rick's made his choice to return to the world, beautiful friendship begun. And McKee is close to ending it all, softy singing Sam's song, crooning an off-key "As Time Goes By."

Unlike rest of his time on stage, McKee has sat throughout most of the six-hour screening of this eighty-minute movie, comfortably perched on a chair, looking up at the screen, sweatered elbow slung back on the table beside him. His pleasure in the picture still evident after god only knows how many viewings. He interrupts, but not too often, his discussion of the movie's finer points long and detailed rather than frequent. And when he does interject—to point out dialogue subtleties and slight turns in subplots—there's a new timbre in his voice, an intimacy lacking in the rest of his lecture. There's the sense he'd be doing exactly the same thing alone in his living room, conversing with the monotone screen, content in the company of the well-told tale. And now, out of his chair and bathed in the low glow of end credits, McKee looks happy, unashamed as his voice struggles to capture Dooley Wilson. He's exactly what all of us in the audience want to be, a consummate storyteller unafraid to stand up and sing for his supper.

I'm ready to rise too, to applaud until my hands hurt, and then run out as quickly as possible. Exalted by what I've witnessed, gutted at what I've let pass, I listen to the old man sigh that ageless song, finally comprehending the courage of forty-foot love and how fundamental things apply.

▶

On the trip home, when the in-flight movie comes on, we watch a few of the opening minutes then turn our eyes from the screen, tell each other long stories instead.

Building on the Bones

The coffin lid is open and we are stumbling up and out, into the light Mediterranean haze of another Beirut dawn.

My companions, mostly Ivy League escapees from good schools around the globe, make guttural demands for breakfast, then go off in search of taxis as I hang back and peer down through the ground-level gap left by the retractable roof of B018: the (literally) underground nightclub we've just clambered out of.

This club, close to the site of one of Beirut's more gruesome Palestinian massacres, features huge casket-like chairs lined along the front of the bar. Amazonian exhibitionists up on the counter shimmy with muscles mostly unknown to the rest of mankind. Memorial slab tabletops lie scattered along the edge of the club as dance floor markers. And on top of the tables, dancers, all happily sweating along to the inane boom of "Feline Woman":

Feline woman
She drinks coffee
She drinks tea

. And as I grin once again at the audacious bad taste of B018, it strikes me just how much I admire this city and these people, dancing on gravestones at daybreak.

But then, people have been doing that here for a long, long time, even during the shelling. Excluding the ongoing conflict in the Israeli-occupied south, the Lebanese civil war lasted fifteen years, from 1975 to 1990. Best estimates—and estimates are all that exist—put the death toll at 170,000, with approximately half a million wounded. At least sixty thousand of those injured were children.

Much of the heaviest fighting centred on the capital itself. Home to up to a third of the country's population, and the epicentre of Lebanon's once miraculous economy, Beirut was gradually drained of its civilian population: 1.3 million people in 1975, 300,000 by 1992. Bankrupted by inconclusive conflict, broken by the Israeli invasion and the Aoun War, "The Paris of the Middle East" acquired a new and well-deserved nickname—"Hell on Earth."

"Hello. How are you?"

"Bonjour. Comment ça va?"

"Guten tag. Wei geht's?"

A few days into my visit and I'm getting used to this game—multilingual greetings yelled by perfect strangers. Mostly they're smiling young men engaged in private bets with their companions, trying to figure out where I'm from. The media's characterization of the Lebanese as terrorists means that tourists are still not so common in Beirut, even after nearly a decade of peace.

It is, of course, obvious to any local that my host — a lapsed Canadian currently working at a local English-language paper — and I are not native to this city. A certainty betrayed not only by our sun-beaten appearance and North American accents, but also by the fact we're eagerly pursuing an activity almost unknown around here: walking.

Ten years after the civil war's end it seems that many Beirutis have returned to their city. And judging by the traffic, it appears everybody brought at least one car with them. Beirut is a city on the move. The screech and honk and roar of cars on the street — and sidewalk — never ends, day or night, as people hurtle along on unreliable roads, demonstrating driving habits utterly at odds with the Lebanese's reputation as the highest per-capita consumers of prescription tranquilizers in the world.

Traffic aside, Beirut is probably the safest city I've ever wandered around. In fact, I've been a lot more anxious in some Vancouver suburbs than in Lebanon. This seeming safety isn't surprising though, given the number of Syrian and Lebanese army checkpoints around town.

Likely the biggest hassle unwary tourists might encounter is the "Love Patrol" on the Corniche, the romantic seaside promenade fronting the city. It's a place made for kissing. The Lebanese army routinely patrols the Corniche, eager to disengage couples too openly affectionate for prevailing social convention. An odd task to assign the army, perhaps. But the Lebanese are all-too-aware of what can happen when people step too far out of bounds, sexually or otherwise.

"You see that building over there?" I pry my eyes off the bomb- and bullet-wracked shell of the Holiday Inn, at one time the world's largest, and follow my friend's pointed finger to a deserted grey monolith, something out of 2001. "Future Home of the Beirut World Trade Center" reads the billboard by its side.

"That's the Murr tower," he explains. "It was finished just as the civil war broke out, and it's still the tallest building in Beirut. The joke around here is that it was built specifically so its Maronite Christian snipers would have a better vantage point than anyone else."

We are standing in what was once the hotel district of Beirut, at the east end of the Corniche. We've been walking around this city for days now, pursued relentlessly by the optimistic horns of private taxis. On our hikes, we've rambled up and down and back and forth across the Green Line, into Christian East, Muslim West, and the Southern suburbs. We've seen the lively café society of Hamra, and the pristine beauty of the American University of Beirut; the dead-zone stillness of the downtown reconstruction district, and the bustling street life of bombed-out tenements.

Block after ever-changing block we walk, moving from high-end shops to devastated hovels in a matter of minutes; through choked streets and an endless and truly post-modern mishmash of architectural styles, each reflecting different periods of occupation: Ottoman, French, occasionally Roman, all the way up to the Bauhaus high-rises of independence.

And, now, in front of the Murr tower, sweaty, disoriented,

exhausted, I think how much I'd give to be swept to its top, gaining a clear view of this city, and finally find out exactly where the hell I am.

Getting lost is easy in Beirut. Before Canada Post began reforming the Lebanese postal service, street addresses had lapsed into disuse. Even now, visitors literally learn to read the different sections of this city: an essential skill in the not-so-far-off days of flying checkpoints, when the wrong time, place, and religion could easily lead to a bullet in the head. Maronite, Sunni, Shiite, Druze . . . there are seventeen major and minor religious sects in Lebanon, and at least as many political affiliations. And by walking through Beirut, I learn to recognize the different signs and insignia of various strongholds: the St. Maron shrines of the largest Christian sect; the clenched fist and Kalashnikov rifle of Hezbollah; the huge posters of President Assad fronting Syrian military housing; the striped cedar flags of Lebanese army checkpoints. Stencilled martyrs are everywhere. Identity is everything.

One belief system changes to another in the space of a block. And in this close, cramped jangle is a sense of how awful the civil war really was. There is recognition of the truth of the refrain heard at the end of almost every war story: "If you weren't here when it was happening, you cannot even imagine."

It is a history that is becoming harder to imagine with the passage of time and the reconstruction of Beirut's devastated downtown — one of the biggest urban renewal projects in the world.

As befits its size, over 1.8 million square metres, the project's official name is a mouthful: The Lebanese Company for the Development and Reconstruction of Beirut Central District. Generally it's called by its French acronym, "Solidere" or, jokingly, "Hariri," after the billionaire politician, Rafiq Hariri, who drove the project into being in 1994.

With a projected cost of over one billion U.S. dollars, the downtown core will eventually be remade into something very much like its former self: an elegant mix of commercial, governmental, and residential buildings. For the most part this is not a preservation project — too many buildings were too badly damaged to be saved. Most of Solidere will be entirely new. Vast and complex, the project is also a shouted announcement to the financially secure members of the global village: Beirut is back and ready for business.

In the middle of Solidere, in this eternity of brand-new buildings, the old comparisons to Paris start to make sense. There is the same inspired creativity and monumental scale. The district is a marvel of how much can be done in so little time; yet consistent with what I've seen elsewhere in Beirut: people pounding down the casket of the past.

Despite its vastness, the full achievement of the ongoing reconstruction project comes up slowly on approach. First glimpses are visible through a no man's land of empty lots and civil war eyesores. Then a forest of construction cranes and shadowy buildings appears under heavy scaffolding.

Finally, the scaffolding falls away and the architecture uni-
fies into pastel pastiche of stonework and glass, and you find
yourself in an airy seaside city full of greenery and open
squares and perfectly maintained streets. It is a surprise, like
a looking-glass mirage. An antiseptic desert rising out of a
surrounding sea of life. Generic, anonymous, solidly without
a sense of self, the clean dream of the reconstruction centre
wouldn't look out of place in dozens of North American cities:
Toronto or San Diego or Vancouver. More Brasilia than
Beirut, Solidere inspires a sense of awe and Oz — the feeling
of being somewhere that somehow doesn't quite exist.

It is also very, very odd. There is an eerie, post-neutron
bomb aspect to the reconstruction district — but the bones
have been cleared away. Solidere stands as more of a
monument to the civil war than any of the mortar-beaten
buildings left standing. This is a downtown without a rush
hour. Or a crowd. It is, as yet, almost entirely uninhabited.
More anticipation than anything else, Solidere is a city
waiting to happen.

Everything associated with Beirut city life — the constant
traffic noise, the never-ending hustle of the street, the ever-
present insignias of identity — is missing. The English language
signs here usually signal things yet to appear, and the only
sounds are the muffled beats of sporadic construction, and
occasional conversation from foreign guest workers.

And when I look at these vast blocks of empty buildings,
I'm left wondering what on Earth they have to do with the
lively city that surrounds them.

But perhaps that's the point. Solidere is about perception, not people. And when they've gotten in the way, they've usually been pushed aside. One of the uglier chapters in Solidere's early history was the mass expropriation of properties from owners — and the consequent expulsion of families — who couldn't afford renovation costs. They became, in the reconstruction company's own odd euphemism, "compulsory partners" and were offered shares as compensation. The future value of these shares is uncertain.

The dead haven't fared so well either. Throughout its construction, Solidere has been dogged by accusations of wanton destruction of archeological sites of international significance. Lebanon has been inhabited since the Stone Age, and as reconstruction workers dig through the strata below downtown Beirut they've discovered evidence of all the city's historical periods, from Canaanite to Crusader, Byzantine to French Mandate. Archeologists have demanded time to properly examine these excavations, but bull-dozers have often cut their studies short. You can't stop for the past when you're in a hurry for the future.

If you build it, they will come. In the rush to negate the recent history of the civil war and prepare a safe, familiar face for the international commercial interests that once made Beirut the financial centre of the Middle East, Solidere has turned the downtown into something as foreign to Lebanon as I am. The reconstruction district is like Oz's Emerald City, existing in some mythical country, somewhere off the map and outside of time — the past unacknowledged, the present uninhabited, the future expected, but of uncertain arrival: no one knows if Beirut will ever possess its prewar prosperity again. And behind the curtain of this particular Emerald City is the attractive illusion that history is something you can escape.

▸

The light is fading, and we are scrambling under a highway overpass on our way to something my friend calls "just a little different."

"Here it is," he says, ducking into a darkening alley. I follow, automatically looking up to find an identifying flag: Clenched fist. Kalashnikov. Hezbollah.

Bang.

Partway down the constricted alley some boys are playing, throwing discarded vegetables at one another. Most of the time they miss, and the vegetables hit parked cars with the fleshy thunk of ripe tissue on tin.

Bang.

"The first time I came through here at night," my friend calls back to me, "I thought it was a little freaky."

"Uh-huh," I answer, non-committal.

Lights are coming on in the apartments crowding the alley, and I can see silhouettes move in front of hanging bulbs. The flicker of incandescent light mingles with the dusk, making the buildings' walls stand out. They look diseased, gouged, like they've been bitten by giant jaws and too-sharp teeth. Clearly, reconstruction money hasn't reached this area. I'm certain most tourists haven't either.

"Hello. How are you?" a voice calls. I look around. There are people all over the sides of the street, relaxing in cooling air, drinking small cups of Turkish coffee. Some smile, some just stare.

Bang.

"Hello," the voice calls out again. But I'm not playing that game today. I'm too engrossed with what's going on inside my head. A mental movie is unreeling, a war film cobbled out of the collective unconscious of the hundred-channel universe. It is full of dead marines and suicide bombers, militia massacres and kidnapped journalists. Right now it's featuring the gaunt face of Terry Anderson. They had him for seven years. He saw the sun once the whole time.

There is no way I'm letting anyone here know where I'm from.

"Of course, this neighbourhood's perfectly safe," says my friend. And I know if I stop, and just answer those "hellos," I'll experience the truth of his assertion. I've been here long enough to be certain that I'd receive the genuine welcome and generous hospitality so typical of this city, no matter how poor the neighbourhood. That within a few minutes of chatting, I'd be swamped with endless offers of American cigarettes and cups of Turkish coffee.

But the skeletons of memory are just too strong to clamp a lid on the horrors stored inside. Shamefaced, I scoot past my friend, blocking out what's around me, dancing away from people I profess to admire. I'm quick-marching towards the future—down to the far end of the block, where in distant streetlights I can see new buildings, in what I think is Solidere, pulled forward by the sight of something familiar, the illusion of greater safety, and the empty promise of what might be.

The Red Queen's Race

We stand on my balcony on the eighteenth floor of my apartment in Burnaby, Andy and me. It's a fall day, early September, and there's a slight breeze filled with the taste of autumn. But it's still warm and clear and we can see for miles, right across the delta, and out at the ocean and islands on the horizon.

Andy leans against the railing, smiling slightly at me. "You know, sometimes when I'm in high places like this I get this uncontrollable urge to jump off," he says.

I fight my own sudden urge to tell him about the guy in my building who did exactly that: jumped off the fifteenth floor. I knew the man slightly, mostly through rapid chats in the suspended time of quick elevator rides. He was unemployed, and liked Asian films, brought stacks of them home from the well-stocked library branch just around the block to kill time during the day. We were both big Kurosawa fans and we'd trade notes about the ones we'd watched until he'd reached his floor. I'd advised him to avoid *Red Beard*. A misstep—both dull and cloying—as far as I was concerned. He'd told me to get my eyes on *Stray Dog* as soon as I could. Then I heard through the building's fecund grapevine that he'd killed himself a short while ago: slit his wrists, then his throat— finally flinging himself off the balcony in a fit of depressed determination. Never did quite catch his name.

Instead, I gently suggest to Andy that we step out of the breeze, go inside and brew some strong coffee while he tells me what it's like to take the leap and live overseas.

Nobody wanted us; university graduates, that is. In the dull economics of the recessed early '90s, a bachelor's degree—the preceding generation's golden ticket to the good life—meant next to nothing in the job market, business majors notwithstanding. For many, four years spent slaving away in the Liberal Arts added up to not much more than a big gap in your job history: time that could have been better spent getting a real trade like making Big Macs or slinging coffee. In most of North America, nothing much was happening. All the real money, all the opportunities, lay elsewhere, across the oceans.

And so they went, my gutsier friends, to begin new lives around the globe: off to the Middle East, some to Europe, many—like Andy and Kim and Bob and Paul—to China and the mini-dragons. Off to start delayed careers by teaching English in Japan and Taiwan and Hong Kong, off to make some decent money, save face, and finally escape the endless question of why they bothered to spend all that time in school.

Andy likes South Korea, for the most part. Works at a language school in a Seoul suburb, and lives in a subsidized apartment close by. The school itself is a little run down, but the students are uniformly diligent, adamantly determined to conquer English despite its vast array of odd idioms and idiosyncrasies. The kids there work way harder than the ones here, no surprise to anyone ever sentenced to a local high school.

There are difficulties, of course: loneliness, and the usual thousand daily struggles of trying to get along in a strange culture. After three years he still can't figure out Korean bank machines. The work is hard, he'd expected that, but the money makes up for the effort, greatly exceeding what he'd anticipated. Makes a decent wage at the school, and even more tutoring at students' homes. He says that tutoring is where all the real cash is. Kids come to the first day of class with fistfuls of yen, determined to bag a teacher for after-school ESL study.

Still, home is home, and Andy's back in Canada, revelling in clean air, familiar faces, hockey nights, and elbowroom. Been here for three months, trying to parlay his Korean stint into an entry-level teaching gig. Must have sent out at least fifty resumes, all accompanied by stacks of sterling referrals, but no bites yet. Apparently, employers here regard overseas jobs as suspect: they want teaching degrees and a long history of gainful employment on closer shores, rather than real experience in foreign trenches.

Andy's running low on cash, and his options are getting pretty narrow, basically down to two: back to school for an education degree to give him the credentials for a nonexistent job that he's already overqualified for, or back to Korea. The term's already started but he's sure his old school would find a job for him. He's not sure he wants to return though.

"It's not the work, or the kids, or even Korea that bothers me," he says. "It's the other teachers."

He tells me a few scandalous stories about the old hands, the expatriates who got there early and then stayed way past their stale dates. How distance releases strange appetites and sets roaming hands free. He's worried about ending up like them—forgotten, jaded, and strange.

"They're degenerates and drunks and worse," he says. "All of them too far from home, and no one around to say no."

▶

In conclusion, I want to say how very, very sorry I am. I want to go to the bank manager and apologize to him in person. I want to tell him I know in my heart that doing fraud is a terrible thing, and I prom-ise never to do it again.

"Finished? Okay, let's see . . . excellent, Willis. You've sum-marized your major ideas, and made a logical conclusion based on those points. 'Doing fraud' is a little awkward, you could use 'committing' or even 'forging cheques' instead, but over-all this is good—it'll probably keep you out of jail. See, I told you all those five-paragraph essays would pay off . . . ."

Like Andy, I'm an ESL tutor, but my Asian gig is right here, in the Lower Mainland. A brief ad for a private instructor led to five years of pressed commutes and after-school lessons in my own personal Golden Triangle, teaching English to a long line of Taiwanese students living in Richmond, North Vancouver, and Burnaby. Five years of grammar primers, provincial exams, laboured essays, LPI and TOEFL tests. Of attempting to clarify the proper use of prepositions, parse continuous tenses, and decode the half-bright word play of tabloid headlines. Half a decade of revisiting lessons and reading novels I disliked when I first encountered them twenty years ago in Grade 12. I must have gone through *Lord of the Flies* fifty times by now. Lord, how I hate William Golding.

Willis looks upset at my mention of prison, his eyes squeezed in worry and the welling push of regret. I explain once again why I don't think he'll see the inside of a cell.

"You've written a letter for the judge just like your lawyer advised, and this is your first offence. You're a good kid, you're in school, working hard, and besides, it wasn't a lot of money . . . was it?"

A tear slithers off a downcast chin. "Two thousand. I wanted to buy a ticket home."

"Two thousand dollars? Of your parent's money? Oh man, your dad's going to kill you when he gets here."

Most of my student's dads are absent. Earning money back home in Keelung, Taitung, or Taipei. They send their wives and kids out here, largely in the hopes of getting the kids into university. The competition for slots in good post-secondary schools is so fierce at home that middling students don't stand a chance, unless they bail and go to a school overseas. So the kids come here carrying heavy but straightforward expectations: learn English, get a degree, and then go back to Taiwan to take over the family business, whatever that may be. All in all, it's a lot of work to get back where you started from.

As for the moms, they're mostly of the stay-at-home persuasion, running the house, and keeping young noses perennially applied to the proverbial grindstone. They don't see their husbands much, and usually don't seem to mind. At least, I've never heard one complain about an absent spouse. For the most part, the mothers seem to get more uptight when the fathers come for visits, usually during the holidays or when, as in Willis' case, someone busts loose and steps too far off the chosen path.

We've got some time left, and I try half-heartedly to get Willis back onto our usual subjects — "So if the fire symbolizes hope, and the conch symbolizes democracy, what do you think Piggy's glasses stand for?" — but neither of us is really into the lesson. Willis has way bigger things to worry about — his dad's plane is due at eleven tonight — and I'm getting sick of living the same routine as my émigré pupils.

I reassure Willis once again about his chances of future freedom, and head out of there early. I'm supposed to catch up with Andy again tonight anyhow. He wants to grab a few beers, pick my brains about trying his hand as a private tutor here before making his mind up about Korea. I drive a few blocks, then turn onto a back road. It's a shortcut to the highway that I discovered just the other day. I don't know this road well, and it's dark and raining, and I can't make out that much through my windshield, just the streaming red glow of a lone set of taillights ahead. I hit the gas, attempt to charge up behind and let someone else guide my way out of here, but they gather speed, disappear behind a crest, leaving me alone and searching for an exit at high speed.

Hello Kitty, Goodbye Wallet

. . . the expression of respect and love is the basis of Sanrio's "Social Communication" business. . . . Whether one is sad, down, happy, or whatever. . .We want to help people share these important feelings with one another. This is the reason for our business. And it is a business of which we are very proud.

— Excerpt from Sanrio's statement of
corporate philosophy

"**S**o what's that?" I inquired, gesturing at the white plastic figurine on my student's desk. "Some sort of insect?"

Sandy's seven-year-old eyes opened in astonished amusement at my question — further confirmation of the astounding ignorance of anyone over twelve.

Looking closer, I tried again: "Oh, I see, it's a caterpillar. No, wait, a rat."

Sandy grabbed up the figurine in a protective cuddle. "Don't you know?" she exclaimed in the exasperated voice of the already enlightened. "It's Hello Kitty!"

And then came the kicker, the Sanrio mantra; the little phrase I've heard over and over again in the eight-odd years since I first encountered the only cat that really matters to more people than you might think; the righteous and largely rhetorical question: "Isn't it cute?"

Well, no, not really. Or at least not in my own grumpy-old-man aesthetic, more generally known as "good taste." To be frank, the sight of a bow-ribboned, button-eyed, mouthless, anthropomorphic kitten dressed in pink inspires me, and perhaps the SPCA, to shivers rather than smiles. Hello Kitty's cuteness quotient alone is likely to induce a diabetic coma in anyone of legal driving age. Yet what's equally clear, and more to the point, is that what I think doesn't really matter. With over twenty-five years of success, and a billion dollars in worldwide sales last year, Hello Kitty doesn't need to catch me in its claws. After all, it's already got your kids.

One of the more dubious joys of teaching English as a Second Language is the acquisition of an intimate knowledge of what passes for "must-haves" in the weird and ever-changing galaxy of pre-teen trends. During my time as a private ESL tutor, I've sat through endless extrapolations involving the evolution of the Pokemon universe; learned far too much about Sailor Moon's saccharine yet determined struggle to stamp out all the world's evil; endured the incessant beeps of electronic Tamagotchi, those endlessly needy virtual space creatures which—for a time—seemed to inhabit virtually every child's pocket; and suffered the songlike stylings of far more flavour-of-the-second adolescent Asian pop stars than I ever care to admit. Yet while these fads have short shelf-lives, the quarter-century-old Kitty's appeal has well outlasted the proverbial nine. The orifice-deficient feline may not have a mouth, but Hello Kitty's got legs. And, increasingly, it's stretching those legs into North America.

▶

I am standing in what may well be the pinkest place on earth: the officially sanctioned Sanrio Surprises store in Metrotown, a mega-mall that seemingly comprises about half of Burnaby, British Columbia. Numbering around two hundred in the U.S. alone, the Sanrio chainstores are the exclusive dens of all the oddly shaped animals released for public consumption by the giant Japanese corporation. With the exception of counterfeits—and promotional give-aways like the ones that prompted line-up fistfights at a number of Taiwanese McDonalds recently—you simply can't purchase their limited edition character products any-where else. If you want to buy something more than a little cute, this is where you come.

And the entire big-headed, button-eyed Sanrio "social communication" clan is here: Winki Pinki, Spottie Dottie and Picke Bicke. Over there, there's Pochacco and Pekkle, and Keroppi the frog. There's Badtz-Maru, a penguin creature, whom I first mistook for an owl. And My Melody, a Red-Riding-Hood rabbit, and those angelic siblings Little Twin Stars, far from their birthplace: Compassion Planet in Dream Galaxy.

But, mostly, inevitably, there is Hello Kitty. Dozens of assorted size plush dolls stare down from the shelves, all benignly blank-faced in the cheerful anticipation of increased social communication and the possibility of an impulse purchase. Although occasionally outfitted in blue attire—a nod to Hello Kitty's much smaller male market segment— it's obvious that the feline's favoured fashion choice is Sanrio pink, a shade approximating the paint colour used in cooling-off cells for calming violent prisoners in our more progressive prisons.

Rita Ho, the Sanrio Surprises store manager, kindly inducts me into the mysteries of Hello Kitty while waiting on a steady stream of customers.

"I think people like Hello Kitty so much because it's so simple, and so cute," she says as she shows me around her store. "Also, the products are of a very high quality."

And the range of products Ho refers to is staggering. Currently the Hello Kitty image graces over 15,000 consumer goods either made or licensed by the cat's parent company, Sanrio. As well, as part of the company's extraordinary marketing strategy to keep its characters fresh, at least another five hundred new Sanrio limited edition items appear every month, the bulk of them Hello Kitty collectibles. Besides the ubiquitous stuffed dolls, backpacks, and hair barrettes, Hello Kitty's under-featured face can be found on food items, toaster ovens, fashion accessories, envelopes, and all sorts of stationery and school supplies. It's there on television sets and cell-phone covers, T-shirts and dish sets, bathroom carpets and candy

JIM OATEN ▸ 123

boxes. Useless trinkets and household appliances for arrested adolescents of every age group. Whatever the surface, this Kitty can cover it with its all-ages cross-cultural appeal.

"When we first started here," says Hong Kong native Ho, "about eighty percent of our customers were from Hong Kong. Now it's about fifty-fifty North American and Asian."

Ho rings in a customer and goes on to add, "Even when we were in Hong Kong, we knew we'd grow with Sanrio together."

Grow up *with* as well. In Asia, and especially Japan, the company has been an institution since it first introduced the Hello Kitty character in 1974. Little more than six whiskers and a hair-ribbon, the image took off with youngsters, making Sanrio's founder, president and CEO Shintaro Tsuji, an extremely wealthy man.

Not that profits get a lot of mention on the corporation's official web site. Instead much space is devoted to the slightly vague concept of something called "Social Communication." In his president's message, Tsuji writes that despite the practical realities of everyday life, "people. . .nonetheless find joy and hope in beautiful, fanciful things such as the blooming of a flower or a bird's cheerful song."

After establishing this insight, Tsuji adds his belief that his business puts "importance on the spiritual side of things" by fostering the type of communication that helps "build a bridge between the hearts and minds of people all over the world." A view that the United Nations seemingly endorsed when it elevated Hello Kitty to the august ranks of Ginger

Spice by making the cartoon character a UNICEF ambassador in 1983 and again in 1994.

Despite Sanrio's otherworldly concerns, the company does keep a close eye on the bottom line. After years of focussing almost exclusively on the children's market, the company engineered its current sales boom by creating character product lines of fashion accessories and household appliances commonly used by grown women. By adding its cartoon-character images to such practical items as toaster ovens, Sanrio gave twenty- to forty-year-old women who grew up with Hello Kitty both nostalgic and "pragmatic" excuses to put the cute cat back into the shopping bag.

Profits increased thirteen-fold in 1998 alone.

►

"Now, I don't collect Hello Kitty," says Ivy Chen, a communications student at Simon Fraser University, "I just buy it."

Nineteen-year-old Ivy is a perfect, if unwitting, example of Sanrio's new target market. She explains how, as a Taiwanese elementary-school student, she and her friends would visit the Sanrio stores weekly—and occasionally daily—to blow their allowances on new Hello Kitty items. She notes how she stopped buying Sanrio "kid stuff" in her teens, but has started picking up a few things again.

"Before when I bought it, there was no reason. Now I just buy the things that can be useful," she says, emphasizing the practicality of her purchase decisions.

We are sitting in the basement in her home, and laid out on the table in front of us is Ivy's Hello Kitty non-collection. There is a Hello Kitty clock and Hello Kitty stationery—if you send a letter with Hello Kitty on it, she explains, people will know it is special and they won't throw it away—and there is an empty Hello Kitty candy box, and a Kitty change holder and a pink air freshener. All useful enough items. And there are other things too, added as Ivy remembers that she owns them: cell-phone antenna decorations and a cup holder and a windshield ornament that works a bit like a yo-yo with the cat on a wind-up string. There's also chewing gum, and some unopened rice flavouring with the cartoon character emblazoned on the packaging. It's too nice to tear, she says.

Other Hello Kittys lurk elsewhere in the house and out in her car, Ivy assures me.

She cheerfully runs upstairs to round them up, and as I'm left alone in that basement staring at the growing pile of Sanrio stuff, it strikes me that maybe I wasn't so wrong when I misidentified Sandy's plastic Hello Kitty as a bug all those years ago. The thing really is as insidious as insect infestation, spreading the consumerist virus to children unequipped to realize that their "special" purchases aren't much more than mass-produced, mass-marketed tat. And that for all of Sanrio's talk of fostering joy, and fun and friendship, of expressing love and respect, there is in the heart of the company something which makes all those fine words as empty as the space where Hello Kitty's mouth is supposed to be.

Ivy's mother comes down, bearing a cup of coffee and questions about what we're doing. I point to the pile on the table and she grins in nostalgic recognition.

"So," I venture, "how about you? Do you like Hello Kitty?"

"Oh, yes, I like it very much," she says. "It's so cute."

Ghosts

t is said, by those that say such things, that July is the month of ghosts in the not-so-far-off East. In every home, red ribbons appear and bowls of food are displayed, each containing only the most succulent of portions. Dues must be paid in July, and the dead demand a meal. It's what they want for being there first. And so their descendants comply—the price of a meal being a good deal for the basis of your own existence, and the clear guarantee those dead in-laws will stay away for yet another year. It is good for butchers, this month, this tossing of chicken bones into the maw of the past.

▶

— Wei?
— Hello, Simon. It's Thomas.
— Hello, I am Simon.

Simon was the youngest and most lucrative of all the Taiwanese students Thomas Mayhew taught privately in the early afternoons and evenings. One of the half dozen Thomas had poached from New Toni's Happy English Learning Academy in a bid to flee the wage-slavery of forced-march grammar tests, and start his own ESL business. One-on-one lessons, seven days a week, anywhere in the Lower Mainland, thirty-five dollars an hour. Simon was more motivated than most, or, rather, his parents were, and Thomas tutored him almost every day.

—Yes, Simon, I know it's you. I phoned you, remember?
Silence.

Simon also had the distinction of being the most stubborn-minded of all the kids he taught. It had taken Thomas weeks to convince the boy that the alien autopsy he'd witnessed on Channel 21 was not, in fact, genuine, even though—as Simon persistently observed—it had appeared on the television news.

—Anyhow, Simon, the reason I phoned is because I can't . . .
—Mr. Tom?
—Umm . . . yes?
—I have a question for you. For school.
—Uh . . . okay. Go ahead. Shoot.
—What?
—It's an idiom. One we haven't done yet. It means . . . go ahead, ask me the question.
—Mr. Tom, what is the evil time?

Thomas shut his eyes and slouched into the receiver, gathering strength for the intuitive leap the question demanded. Usually the hazards of Chinglish translation were easily overcome—god knows he'd had enough practice. But today the sludge of insomnia was making clear thought close to impossible.

Thomas wasn't sure what was keeping him awake. Usually, he slept well in the summer. All that time outside. Fresh air relaxed him. The weather had changed, though, in the last few weeks, pushing him indoors as the city reverted to fleece, drizzle, and the certain belief there was no such thing as the sun.

    —*The evil time? I don't know. Where did you hear this?*
    —*My teacher. Social Studies. And on TV one time. Like the ET. The dead one.*
    —*Please, Simon, not that again, I'm too tired. Let's just stick to Social Studies, okay?*
    —*But I saw it on the news . . .*

He was sure, though, it wasn't just anxiety over the early end of summer spurring his insomnia. He'd lived in Vancouver long enough to be unsurprised by July monsoons. There was the AIDS test his new girlfriend had asked him to take, before things went much further. Certainly, that had put him on edge. Waiting for results really wasn't much fun, yet this had started before he'd visited Doctor Chen.

He wasn't sure when, but lately it seemed to Thomas that something had unfurled in his head, a flap of aural memory that had somehow come unstuck. And every so often it would snout into his consciousness, freezing him in place like an epiglottal stop. In the beginning, he'd only heard this . . . noise . . . every once in a while, in that anesthetic time before the drift of sleep. But now it was waking him almost every night and early morning, a sound torpedo of his intermittent dreams:

Each of his parents had worked an almost equal distance from the house Thomas had grown up in, the one edging the ocean. And, not always, but often enough for it to become commonplace, their after-work arrival would coincide. And on the walk from the carport, up the stairs, to the sliding-glass door leading into the house—that slam, stomp and rolling swish— they would start to fight. As a youngster, as an adolescent, and for a short time after that, he had heard the rough shuffle of mounting anger, knowing full well when it arrived he would be involved, held to account for something: toys left out; dishes undone; water in the whiskey bottle. Whatever was necessary.

And what was waking him was the sound of them, just outside the door, where the sliding glass let anger through, but took the words themselves away. Jerked from sleep by familiar faces and the howl of days-gone-by demand.

—*Simon, you watch too much TV. You should be doing homework.*

—*I am doing homework. On the evil time. It was dark. Everyone look like Xena.*

Dark. Eureka.

—Do you mean the medieval times? The Dark Ages? Were there kings and a lot of sick people around? And it's "looks," not "look."

—Yes, that's right. Medieval times. Tomorrow we get the test on it.

—I think you better go over your notes again . . . anyhow, the reason I phoned is because I want to cancel our lesson today. I have to go to the doctor's. I have an appointment.

No matter how Thomas counted, it still added up to almost everybody. The permutations of sexual history were the mother of all pyramid schemes, as fucking to the power of ten got to about a billion a lot quicker than you'd think.

Okay, he'd thought, just long-term relationships.

Yes, that was it. Simplify the math, and clear off some of the clutter on the path to survival. Just forget about her and her and whatshername: all of those closing-time draught beer beauty queens. And that time in the car, and that time on the grass, and that time when her husband came home and found the three of you. Forget that. And the eighties, they could go. For now, for at least a little bit. And the nineties for that matter. Keep it current, that was the ticket. With the ones you loved. The ones that lasted. Just for the sake of the arithmetic, you understand. It's not ducking anything, avoiding reality, it's just that I can't compute very well, and my calculator isn't handy. Head math is a dying art you know.

Which left that question which was always asked at some point in the progress of love: How many others were there, my dear? Five? Fifteen? Far too many to decently recount?

And when you weren't certain, were you always safe? Were things slipped and sheathed, pinched and rolled, secured against exchange? Did you have dental dams, nonoxynol-9 and the taste of latex at the back of your throat? Safe? Always? Every time?

Of course not.

When he dialed the phone to return the doctor's call this morning, Thomas's palms were slick, moist with the effort of memory and the bony clasp of other people's lovers.

Pause — *What time you coming, Mr. Tom?*

He'd only known one AIDS victim. Someone who was HIV-positive or T-cell deficient or whatever the current euphemism was — hell, he didn't even know if people still died from it. Didn't Magic Johnson have a talk show? An infomercial? He'd only watched one person ending in front of his eyes. Doug, the boyfriend . . . partner . . . companion of an old high school friend.

— Jesus, listen to me, Simon. I said no class. I'm going to the doctor's.

Never seen Doug looking really ill either, not over the two years he'd known him. A slight pallor, perhaps. Complaints of tiredness. Occasional, unexplained disappearances. Something that might have been a lesion. But then he'd never wanted to get to know him that well either. Didn't want to risk that pain. Or, at least, that's what he told himself.

—So you coming early, right?

—Simon, remind me to give you more conversation practice.

—What?

—Nothing . . . it's not important . . . just listen carefully, okay? I am not coming today. No class today. You are free, understand? No class.

—Oh! I am free. No class, yes?

—Yes, Simon, yes.

The refrigerator door is open and Doug is pulling out pills and a jug of what looks like chocolate milk. "Just let me take these," he says, counting out capsules, "then we'll get out of here." Thomas has swung by Doug's apartment to give him a lift to the movies. Everybody's going and Doug has been invited by default. Friend of a friend sort of thing, and Thomas lives the closest.

It's a small apartment with no division between the kitchen and the living room. It's also the first time Thomas has been here, and he's . . . *4, 5, 6* . . . looking around, taking in the posters, and pictures, and knickknacks . . . *10, 11, 12* . . . and trying not to look into the other room, the kitchen. Trying not to see how Doug is struggling with the pills now . . . *17, 18, 19* . . . yet hearing the forced bob of his Adam's apple set a gasping rhythm: *Swallow. Pump. Retch. Cough.* The choke of chicken bones and history at bay.

—Mr. Tom?

—Yes, Simon.

A giggle *—If I am free, then you are free too.*

Doug died a short time after that. Not infection, though. A Parisienne. Dropped the car on top of himself while trying to fix its linkage. Wanted to get it running right, so he could get out to an AIDS rally in Victoria. And when Thomas's friend had phoned with the news . . . *What? I didn't even know he was in hospital* . . . they had howled with laughter at how it had all ended.

Giggle — *You are frrreee!*

▶

The bank machine, and his local smoke shop. The security zone at the SkyTrain station. Three more and he'd make his quota; help perpetuate Vancouver's claim to world-class status. Thomas had read, somewhere, that the inhabitants of every major Western city were photographed at least six times a day as they went about their business. The factoid had stuck with him, and now he always counted on any cross-town trip. It bothered him a little too, the thought of all those frozen moments, filed away god-knows-where, just waiting for the light of late-breaking news and Crime Stoppers specials.

Thomas supposed there were pictures of himself here as well: X-rays, and that mole photo Dr. Chen had taken a couple of years ago. Voluntary privacy invasions likely didn't count though, except as a distraction.

Never without a condom again. Ever.

—Hello, Mr. Mayhew, sorry to keep you waiting. Just let me check your chart here, make sure we're on the same page. Wouldn't want to mix you up with another patient, take out some of your parts by mistake . . . ha, ha . . . oh, that's right, test results.

Dr. Chen never aged. Not a wrinkle on the man.

—Now the reason I've brought you down here, and I hope my secretary mentioned this when she left a message earlier. . .

Couple of grey hairs, maybe. Thinning a bit. Can't remember if he had those glasses. Awfully soft-spoken. Getting hard to hear. Hard to breathe.

. . . is that I never give HIV test results over the phone, especially with answering machines. Can get a little sticky, if you know what I mean . . . ha, ha . . . what's that? Insomnia? Yes, you are looking a little run-down. I could prescribe something if you want . . .

Christ. Breathe. Listen.

. . . of course, you might sleep a bit better after you hear this. Now you'll have to take this test again in six months, just to make sure, but the preliminary results of your test say . . .

You are freee!

A rising chorus. An angelic tide, carrying him out of the

office, down the stairs—foolish for a healthy man to take an elevator, after all, what's six flights—and under the unseen eye of the lobby security cam. Out the door, around some tourists. Light feet slipping off a rain-soaked sidewalk. Into the sound of screeching brakes.

. . . No pain, just twitching neurons spurting trivia—trying to get all that stuff out, one last time, in the desperate hope it'll finally be useful. A tangled purge of old algebra lessons, celebrity birthdays and the taste of Crayola crayons. But Thomas is well away from irrelevance now. Rising towards light and dim figures—the shadowy outline of what looks like his parents. Closer and clearer, he can make out their features. Mouths moving around smiles as they catch sight and beckon. Words finally forming as he moves into the white light of . . .

. . . fifty flashbulbs going off at once. Nikons and Canons and cardboard cameras poked out of tour-bus windows; package travellers capturing a near miss and the big-game bonanza of a body crumpled right in front of them. Trembling, groggy, unhurt except for a swelling bump on the side of his head, Thomas rolls away from the twee double-decker, and onto his feet, an I'm-okay smile stuck on for the shaken driver, yet silently seething; enraged at clumsy feet and lost face. Falling down in front of tourists. Amusing all those postcard-grabbers. Entertaining strangers who still believed in stupid things like ghosts.

Accelerated Paces

Voi

Beneath our wheels, the ragged slide of deep ruts and red soil. Above us, the southern sky and the rolling splendour of night undiminished by urban lights. On either side, five thousand acres of sisal plants, their dry poles stretching out of low spiky leaves, ready to seed at the end of the growing season.

In the back of the truck, Kiseru, Jaspert, and me. We're braced against the clattering cab, hanging on to spotlights mounted on top of the roll bar. We fire shaky beams at the endless fields flying past, watching for the feral reflection of animal eyes.

Every few minutes the speeding truck hits a crumbling pothole, and we all yell with undisguised pleasure as our feet lift from pitted steel and into small orbits ... *Aiyee* ... *Aiyee* ... *Yee haw*. Our lights shoot into the sky as we thump back down, bodies bumping in the truck's erratic sway. Kiseru's leather-sheathed machete — the ever-present *panga* hanging from his belt — smacks against my leg. He's the head of security for the farm.

We're out here, on this god-awful road in the middle of an East African night, looking for elephants. The farm—the sisal plantation—belongs to my wife Anar's family. It's sandwiched between two wings of a huge national park, Tsavo East and West, and animals are always getting in, drawn by water and the lure of oranges and melons growing in the plantation's horticulture section. Usually, it's just baboons, giraffes, or zebras, the occasional herd of Cape buffalo, but tonight there's a good chance that elephants have breached the farm's perimeter. A section of electric fence is down, and workers have seen tracks. They're hugely destructive, elephants, and if they're around they'll need to be driven out.

Of course, moving elephants about is beyond my admittedly limited skill set, although Shakil—Anar's brother and the truck's driver—says he knows how to do it: a fairly straightforward procedure that involves car horns, provocation, and the judicious use of reverse gear. And Kiseru's pretty much ready to take on anything as long as he's got his *panga*. But I've already declared my absolute refusal to be involved in anything as insane as wild-elephant wrangling at midnight. I've been on enough safaris to understand just how big, fast, and dangerous the damn things are. Besides, our strict mandate is to simply report, not reposition, and I'm just fine with that.

A hiss of excitement. Kiseru bangs his back against me, whips his spotlight around. He's seen something—gleaming eyes and a low shape crouched by the side of the road. Shakil sees it too, and slows the truck, crawls up to get a closer look.

It's a tiny antelope—a dik-dik—fully grown and about a foot and a half high. I can see shivers convulsing its soft grey coat as we pull up beside it, our spots holding the terrified animal in place.

"*Tembo ndogo*," snickers Kiseru.

"Small elephant," translates Jaspert.

We watch the dik-dik shiver for a few more minutes, then snap off our lights, set it free, bounce back up to speed.

Anar pops her head out the passenger side window and shouts back at us. "They're just up the road. We'll drop off the chai, and then head back."

Her Dad's been out here for a few hours, working with his crew at one of the farm's many small generators, trying to get power back to the electric fence. I can hear the putting clank of the generator cutting above the low-gear grind of engine noise. Lights and a ramshackle hut swing into view. A few men hanging around the ancient Toyota parked outside.

The truck slides to a halt, and Anar and Shakil trundle out with a couple of thermoses and a covered plate of cooling samosas. They go inside and a few moments later the generator cuts off, plunging us into the lively hum of the nocturnal world. Everywhere I can hear the water-sprinkler snicks of what I think are cicadas, marking territory and calling for mates. There's something else too, a rhythmic chunk far off in the distance, echoing across the fields. It's the sound of someone chopping wood.

It's probably a trespasser, a charcoal burner collecting fuel for his trade. You can see them all over Kenya, perched on top of rows of bursting gunnysacks stored under shade trees along the highways. They do a brisk trade with truck drivers needing briquettes for cooking fires on long journeys. The high demand has led to rapid deforestation though, especially in this semi-desert area, and burners often sneak on to the farm after dark to fell trees in fallow fields.

Kiseru turns his head in the direction of the axe falls, bloodshot eyes scanning distance and night, then says something in Swahili too fast and rich for me to follow. Jaspert interprets, a half grin stretching his words' slow precision. "He says that's the sound of Shaitan. That's the Devil out there chopping wood."

The old man watches my face, deadly serious as Jaspert recounts his explanation. He's the spookiest man I've ever met, Kiseru, and I'm not particularly surprised by this latest glimpse inside the dark recesses of his head. Whenever I've spent any time with him he's told me at least one highly disturbing thing. The first story was relatively mild in retrospect: a small tale about a furry fish he caught that mewled and shrieked until he threw it back into the water. The latest story—the one he told Jaspert and me last night about the head he picked off the railway tracks after a homebrew bash went wildly wrong—gave me nightmares.

Overall, I'm just grateful he's on my side, quietly patrolling the farm on his bike, keeping me safe while I don't sleep at night.

Kiseru continues his explanation, gesturing at his feet

with odd emphasis, pausing as Jaspert patiently takes up interpreter duties once again. I notice the grin is gone from his face.

"He says that when Shaitan comes close, when the Devil wants to get right beside you, he'll wear the body of a friend or a family member. He will look exactly like those people. There is one way only that you can tell the difference. You must look at the shoes. Shaitan's feet face backwards."

Kiseru nods. Points downwards. No devils here. Just desert boots, calloused toes, and rough sandals made of old tire treads.

The generator kicks on again, and light freezes us all for a moment, each staring at one another's startled faces, our quiet surprise broken by a banging door as Anar and Shakil emerge and walk back towards the truck. As they come closer I can't help but look at their feet.

They clamber in, fire up the truck, and we rattle off into the night, shining lights and searching for life.

Florence

Death stalks the piazza, hunting lira, dollar, rupee, and pound. In the middle of all this Renaissance glory, a medieval apparition: a scuttling black shroud keening for alms in an unknown tongue. The figure is shapeless, yet still recognizable as a woman of sorts. She passes close by and we can see brown eyes slinking from behind a slitted veil, picking likely targets.

Her heavy-soled shoes—like those worn to correct club-feet—clack as she scurries towards milling tourists in the square, outstretched hands wrapped in filthy bandages.

I turn to Quilty. "So whaddya think? Leprosy?"

He considers, long fingers twiddling eyebrow's end.

"Eczema, more likely."

I laugh and we leisurely sip our seven-dollar coffees, the exorbitant price guaranteeing ringside seats and the shade of a patio umbrella. Behind us, paunchy men lean against smooth marble countertops, gulping down espressos in the manner of true Italians everywhere.

The beggar staggers towards a clean-cut couple. They startle away in fear, throwing coins in their wake like talismans warding off an evil eye.

Quilty reconsiders. "Elephantiasis, perhaps?"

A shriek now, a crying child swept away from the looming spectre.

"Think there's a lot of money in that? Terrifying children?" I ask.

"Works for teachers...she seems to be doing okay."

We watch as scooped coins disappear deep inside her clothes.

"I've seen it before, you know," I say.

"Seen what?"

"Elephantiasis. In Kenya, mostly on the coast. You'd see people with it on the street sometimes. They'd have these huge legs and the flesh just kinda puddles around their feet."

"Jesus—any cure?"

"Not that I know of. Poor bastards. It was another reason I'd coat myself in DEET when I was there. I heard you could get it from a mosquito bite…anyhow she doesn't have it—she's way too skinny."

"AIDS then."

"Maybe…better to have elephantiasis."

We sit in comfortable silence as the beggar switches to a less energetic tactic. She squats, furls into a low tattered mound, waits for tourists too engrossed in the splendid architecture around them to trip over her before springing up with indignant demands for money.

"Man, she's way too freaky for this."

Quilty grunts mild agreement, lips pursed around a newly lit Marlboro Red.

It's taken ten years of friendship and two months of planning to bring us to this place. I've arrived via a short family visit in the U.K., and Quilty's made his way to Italy from his current home in Lebanon. Haven't seen him since he escaped a crushing student loan by fleeing to the Middle East a few years back, but we've travelled well together over the last couple of days, moving through the country like an island of two—familiar rituals and company tricking us into feeling like we're still in our element and somewhere close to home.

"God, what's she doing now?"

The beggar's on her knees, shuddering in a grand mal grip. Her hands clutch at each other spastically, pulling off blackened wrappings to the accompaniment of low throaty moans. She staggers to her feet, twirls and kicks off thick shoes as everyone around skitters, stops, and watches from a safer distance. Dark fingers grab bunches of black shroud and lift it over her head. Her face finally freed from the thin veil.

Beads of sweat on flawless olive skin. The gypsy teen draws herself to full height, lithe and healthy limbs rippling under her short bright skirt. She drops the shroud and skips off, barefoot through the piazza, laughing at all the fools who ran away and those who gave her money.

We finish our drinks, grab our smokes, and head off to see the rest of the sights. I'd been to Florence a few times before, and irritated by the crowds, slightly bored by the despotic beauty, I rush my friend through everything too quickly.

Quilty refuses to talk to me for the rest of the day.

Vegas

There's a graveyard in Vegas. Out past the north end of the strip where the city dribbles into desert. A boneyard, filled with the near-past relics of old neon signs. It's a holding area for the Neon Museum: three acres full of the extinguished lights of failed hotels, refurbished casinos and long-forgotten roadside attractions, all awaiting resurrection and the blessing of funding ample enough to put them back in easy public view.

There's a defunct Trust in there, decaying slowly in the desert sun, and Sin as well, its letters jovial orange slab serifs.

The Golden Nugget's around somewhere, and a couple of old Burger King signs. There's the uniquely spelled Tropicana Mobil Park, the aquamarine Jackpot Motel, a garish grinning duck, and the sassy promise of the Cheesecake Revue. A huge figure's on the site, draped in rust and '70s garb, stooped eternally over an absent pool table. And a twenty-foot-high silver slipper, sticking out of the sand like the Statue of Liberty at the end of that bad monkey movie. All of it, a low-rent and electricity-free memorial: an unexpected counterpoint to that other isolated Sin City commemoration of emptied wallets, the high-wattage Luxor pyramid at the other end of the strip. They claim that the casino's blue-tinged beacon is visible from outer space.

It's a fairly cheerless view of Glitter Gulch, I know: a long strip in the middle of nowhere bounded by two faux gravesites. But Las Vegas is essentially a mirthless town, even in these last few days before Christmas. Despite the endless invitations to let loose and have fun, all the free liquor and practiced winks at mild indiscretion, there isn't a lot of laughter around here: just the occasional sharp barks of high-rollers hitting it lucky, and the emphysemic chortles of seniors finally getting something back after nine-hour stretches at the nickel slots.

Not that Vegas isn't worth a visit. It's too over-the-top to ever be dull. But the utter relentlessness of the place takes its toll pretty quickly, despite all the oxygenated air and the miles of *trompe l'oeil* blue-sky ceilings. And so here we are, my travelling companion and I, out on a brief escape from the glitzy press of the Strip, looking forward to the quiet respite of dead neon after a couple of days of frenetic casino hopping. The Boneyard's open by reservation only, and our quick research shows that it's not much visited, surprising since the place should be, by all rights, a crowded mecca for Rat-Pack devotees from all over the world—if only they could find the place.

Our taxi driver obviously can't. In fact, he's completely lost. Remarkable since there's really only one main road here. Takes us to a mostly empty spot, just past the down-market casinos on the north end of Las Vegas Boulevard. Insists this is our destination; we're equally insistent it's not. We argue for a few minutes, as he circles the block, meter running, then decide it's better to be uncertain of our whereabouts under our own steam—certainly a lot cheaper—and bail out.

Downtown Vegas—close to fifteen minutes from the centre of the Strip, and about three decades past the days when Sammy would drop by. It's seedy here, and full of poverty's desperate clichés: boarded storefronts and shopping carts, brown paper bags and needy pulls at over-proof bottles. In the near distance, we see Fremont Street, the canopied spectacle of its psychedelic light show reduced to a swathe of stark steel mesh by sun and desert sky.

We spot an open store—a tattoo parlour—and duck inside to ask directions. The shaven-headed proprietor's surprised to see us, and slightly less friendly when we quickly declare that we don't want any ink. He knows the Boneyard though.

Says it's not too far from here, but a bus won't be by for at least another fifteen minutes, and there's no way we'll get a taxi. "Come back at night," he says. "That's when all the tourists are here."

"Besides," he adds, "the odds are better at this end of town."

I doubt that, I think.

We're already half an hour past our Neon Boneyard reservation time, and we decide to skip it, to bus back down into the heart of the Strip. Catch the Deuce — the cheap double-decker bus favoured by locals and the newly poor — and listen to homebound workers bitch about their jobs as we slide past increasingly spectacular pleasure domes. Briefly admire the tacky bronze lion perched outside the MGM Grand, then spot the Tropicana. I've heard that its casino's still relatively untouched by the recent tidal wave of renovations and decide to try my luck, finally get a taste of what the place would have been like for the original *Ocean's Eleven* crowd. I hop off the bus while my partner stays on, tired of chasing the past and ready for an air-conditioned nap behind the tinted windows of our hotel room.

Through the doors and into the stench of old Vegas — fifty years of unfiltered cigarettes, spilled cocktails, and the sweaty residue of dashed hopes. Tired carpets and low, mirrored ceilings reflecting row after row of one-armed bandits, each endlessly chirping dinging chimes. The entire effect of the place is more claustrophobic than classy, similar to being stuck inside a shoebox full of demented Christmas ornaments.

I trawl through the slots, looking for a blackjack machine. Although I know absolutely nothing about gambling, and have no supporting evidence, I'm convinced the odds are better on the blackjack slots. Find one—they're fairly rare—and chuck away fifty bucks in under five minutes. So much for my system.

Decide I'm done, and try to head back to the bus stop. End up getting completely turned around, disoriented in the casino's maze of mirrors, slot machines and the hypnotic swirl of bad carpet. Plunge ahead, following dim aisles full of roulette wheels, rolling dice and inner-sanctum poker tables, each turn taking me deeper inside the Tropicana. I'm lost, and I start laughing out loud at the ridiculousness of it all, at the idea of being trapped—entombed—by this casino. Everyone around me, indifferent, too intent on their own losses to pay attention to the ordinary illusion of an easy way out.

Ikea

It's a birthday party, and in the new tradition of modern parenthood, I deposit my son at the Family Fun Centre and run off to browse the big box stores in the surrounding area. Wander Winners' warren of discarded brand names, then off to the largest dollar store on Earth to view its staggering selection of tat and fine plastics. Skirt the Depots (Office and Home) and resist the draw of Canadian Tire. Finally succumb to the Nordic vortex, get sucked into Ikea and the siren call of clever storage solutions and Swedish meatballs.

Escape after thirty minutes, mildly discouraged by the thought of putting all those things together. Too many Allen keys for my taste. Made pretty good time getting out of there though. Refused to fall into the deliberate maze of tiny rooms and impulse purchases, and took as many shortcuts as I could. Still have a couple of hours to kill before I'm due back. Decide to call my friend Scott from my car in the parking lot. He lives close by, and it could be a good time for a long-delayed visit.

I catch him as he's about to deliver his teenage son to his weekend job. No time for a visit, but enough for a quick catch-up chat on the phone. We talk, a little awkwardly at first, but soon fall into familiar rhythms and the easy domain of commonplace topics: families, sports, and mutual friends; old scandals, new divorces, and recent successes; journeys, far and near, taken and planned; the twin spectres of encroaching middle age—memory lapses and health scares.

"You ever hear of a doctor called Kobyashi?" Scott asks.

"No . . . sounds like a Japanese restaurant."

"He's Indian. Some sort of naturopath. I hear he's pretty famous. I was feeling really stressed a while back and my aunt turned me on to him."

"You gotta stop getting divorced," I say.

"Yeah, those lawyers will kill you."

I watch a family strain to fit a flatpack into their econo-car. There used to be a forest here.

"I make an appointment, go and see this Kobyashi guy, and as soon as I'm in there he bangs a tuning fork against my head, holds a couple vials of stuff near my ears and tells me that my fluids are out of whack. And I'm thinking, no, it's this guy that's totally out of whack, and that it's time to get the hell outta out here."

"Sounds like a good plan to me."

"Yeah, but I trust my aunt, she's not gonna steer me wrong, so I decide I'm going to give this guy a chance, can't hurt, probably. So I stay, and this dude puts down his vials and other witch-doctor shit, and tells me he's going to start counting. Says that when he gets to a certain number he's going to stop because something happened to me at that age. Something significant that I think I've forgotten, but that I've actually blocked, that I've repressed."

All the car doors open now. Baby seat unloaded. They're trying all the angles.

"Kobyashi grabs my hands, which is kind of gay if you ask me, but whatever…I'm trying to be open-minded about this whole thing… and he starts counting, one, two, three, four, five, six…seven, he says, something happened to you when you were seven years old."

Drops on my windshield. It's starting to rain. That cardboard's going to get wet.

"You know me, I can't remember yesterday, let alone when I was seven, and I'm about to tell this old quack to fuck off, when I'm overwhelmed by this memory, this car crash I was in with my Mom when I was seven. Someone plowed into us at an intersection, and I went right through the windshield. And I can remember lying on the road, looking at the sky with my forehead cut all to shit. I'd totally forgotten about it, blocked the whole thing. Then he goes on, eleven this time, and then thirteen, and I'm practically bawling by now with all this stuff coming back to me . . ."

Success. They've finally squeezed the flatpack in. Looks like there's no room for the baby seat. Their kid's outside, crying in the rain.

"As soon I get out of Kobyashi's office, I call my mom and bawl her out for an hour for all the bad things that happened to me as a kid. Not that any of it was her fault . . ."

I sense Scott's story is ending, and I rifle through my memory, scouring continents and time, picking out my own tale of surprise and expectation, ready to complete the ritual exchange of past lives.

"I'm supposed to make another appointment, but there's no way I'm going back to see that guy again. He totally freaked me out."

The flatpack's out of the car now, loaded back onto the low dolly. The family schleps back to the entrance. Shoulders slumped with showers and the expectation of breaking the Swedish store's cardinal rule: a request for home delivery.

"Did I tell you I went to Vegas at Christmas?" But there's no time for my anecdote. Scott's got to go drive his son to his afternoon shift at the hardware store. We make vague promises to see each other soon, half-hearted attempts to angle each other into already full schedules. Both of us know that nothing much will come of our plans, but we're happy enough with this arm's-length substitute for face-to-face contact, for the chance to trade postcards salvaged from life's crush, tell stories drafted by swift pens and accelerated paces.

A Day at the Races

So Scott phones me up a few weeks back, tells me he's scored all these free tickets for Indy, and that he'll be there in ten minutes to pick me up. Okay, I say.

And he comes cruising up like two minutes later in this fucking Porsche he's acquired—I mean this car must cost like sixty grand easy, I guess he does better at his job than I thought he did, I don't know, don't see him that much any more—anyhow, he's got this car and he's totally fucking wired, looks like hell, just had the most debauched thirty-fifth birthday celebration and he's still coming down from the half-pound or so of coke that he and his pals hoovered up the night before.

Man, you should have seen these girls, he keeps saying, all of 'em tens—elevens 'cuz they swallowed.

We've got maybe ten minutes till the race starts, and we gotta get downtown, so I hop in and he drives like a maniac, talking and taking calls the whole time, and I have to keep yanking my elbow back inside the car to keep it from getting chopped off as we rat-race past everything around us in a million-mile-an-hour blur, and my neck twists like a chicken on the chopping block every time Scott stomps the gas which he does every time there's even an inch of space open — I mean it's like a special-needs Indy all the way down to the fucking track, with Scott babbling and stomping and sniffling and me doing the geeky chicken dance like some spaz on the short bus.

We get there, somehow, on time, and pull into our reserved parking spot, that's how good these tickets are, and we head up to the grandstand — silver section, second-most expensive, the whole place smelled like Polo — to watch the race, and we totally lose track of what's going on after about ten laps or so, haven't got a clue who's who or what's going on.

So we decide, fuck it, we didn't pay for this.

There's maybe seventy laps to go, and it's the same thing every lap, might as well get some beer and we head off to the beer garden and we run into this guy Scott knows that can touch his forehead with his tongue, and he does this a few times and we have some beers, and we scope out the Molson Indy Hot Tub Bikini Team, each with their own built-in plastic flotation devices, if you know what I mean, for like an hour or so, until they announce there's only like twenty laps left to go, so we head back to catch the end — I mean it's supposed to be the reason we're here, but instead of going up to our seats, we decide we really want to get into the whole Indy experience.

You know like really feel it.

So we sneak down to the track, right at one of the

corners, to watch the rest of the race, and it's like totally cool, we're right on the edge of the track behind this skinny chain-link fence and all the cars come screeching straight at you and we can't hear a damn thing 'cuz the engines are so fucking loud, it's like your whole heart shakes when the entire pack zooms by, and from where we are we can see right inside the cockpits and watch the driver's heads bobble around like those little plastic wiener dogs you used to see through rear windows in the seventies, and I'm wondering how you can drive and bounce your brains around that fast and not kill anybody.

Anyhow, as you can guess, we're totally enjoying this, Our Indy Experience, until this big fat volunteer woman comes running up and starts yelling at us to move, that this is a Restricted Area for Race Personnel Only, and Scott's arguing with her and she's pushing, and I mean really, actually pushing me, and telling Scott that if he's got tickets he should go and use them, go and sit in his seat, and Scott, who's been pretty edgy the whole day, totally loses it and screams at this poor sweaty woman,

Seats! I know I got seats! I paid three hundred fucking dollars for my fucking seats!

Completely ignoring the fact that we're doing this whole Indy thing for free, the tongue guy even bought us our beers, and Scott's all puffed and red and right in this woman's face and I'm pretty sure he's going to take a swing at her, and she's screeching and signalling and all these security guards come swarming over and the whole thing's getting pretty ugly, and we've lost track of whatever the fuck is going on with the race at this point, with this fat lady screaming at us and all and spoiling the whole thing, our entire Indy Experience, and then we hear the crowd making all this noise . . . everybody's yelling and clapping and howling like monkeys and we look up and, there right beside us on the track, Bobby Rahal, three-time former Indy Champion is on fire, and well . . .

Well, fuck, did we laugh.

CNN and the Heat Death of the Universe

Chunka . . . chunka . . . "Mojo rising" . . . chunka . . . chunka . . .
"Rising. Rising."
Scott beat the martini shaker against the steering wheel, keeping
time as the dead Door wailed away on the stereo.

We were going, as usual, much too fast. The car was a mutant, built by some graveyard-shift assembly-line worker with dreams of greater glory and days of thunder. Its only speed verged on the illegal, but fell well within the range of stupidity as we swept along the rain-soaked streets. Fast and ugly, the squat yellow beast suited our purposes.

Scott snapped off the radio, and turned towards me. He wanted to talk. I began to worry.

"Morrison's dead, you know," he said. "He died in a Paris bathtub at the age of thirty. Or, at least, that's what most people think. Personally, I think it was the CIA . . . but these things are hard to prove . . . sometimes the facts just don't fit the theory. Take quantum mechanics, for example. Just how do you prove those things? Me, I prefer Newtonian physics . . . gravity and stuff like that. Stuff you can actually see. Here, I'll show you."

He slammed on the emergency brake.

ZZZZZZIIIIIIIIINNNNGGGGG . . . greenwhitegreyblack . . . greenwhitegreyblack . . . greenwhitegreyblack . . . the car spun in 360s, headlights highlighting lawn, traffic, concrete, and road. The shaker smashed against the door, filling the car with the fine mist of expensive liquor and me with the certain knowledge we were going to die. Light strobed as we spun across lanes, high beams bearing down on us like the eyes of Ahab focussing on that big fishy bastard after all that time. Squishy fear sounds filled the car.

Then all was normal. The car straight; the spinning gone. The blood roar in my ears began to subside.

Scott giggled. "That," he said, "was centrifugal force."

Sick with the shock of survival, I flopped against my seatbelt as a car boomed past us, headlights flashing, horn blaring. Suspecting a cop, Scott lurched our vehicle towards the curb, then, realizing it wasn't, swore and snarled into the receding taillights. "Some people just can't handle the unexpected."

►

Indeed, some people can't handle the unexpected, and most of us do our damnedest to avoid it: an act which makes infinite sense, especially when you consider that the people we pay to encounter the unforeseen — such as cops, soldiers and foreign correspondents — fail and die with depressing regularity.

Take, for example, the time when Desert Shield squalled into a storm; the exact moment the Americans began the first bombing of Baghdad.

On the station that was on — one of the smaller U.S. border stations that broadcast into B.C. — the information had arrived, but the images hadn't: the scoop just had to be shunted through the anchor who had held the front desk for at least a half a dozen years. You knew this was the moment of moments; that this was going to be the big announcement that the Gulf War had begun after weeks of waiting. It couldn't possibly be anything else: deadlines had passed, programs interrupted, "Special Report" splashed across the screen. All we needed to know now was that it had actually started, and the anchor was our conduit to that confirmation.

So we sat in front of the TV like supplicants before a Sibyl, waiting for words that originated from somewhere unseen, for information that would give us a glimpse of our most immediate future. And the anchor put on his best professional face and he opened his mouth and . . .

. . . and he blew it. He just died. He sat there yammering and stammering, drowning in flop sweat and information overload, desperately trying to stutter out what was the most important story of his career . . . and failing. The story was too big, the news too unusual; he just couldn't handle the unexpected — even when he knew it was coming.

Of course, the anchor did finally manage to make the announcement that the Gulf War had begun, but by then it was too late: we were already switching to CNN in the hope we might see what was really going on. And what we saw there—between the bombs and the self-congratulation of exclusive footage—was a quick glimpse of the Second Law of Thermodynamics and entropy in action.

Entropy is the unexpected. Like centrifugal force, it's a primary concept in the field of physics. Like a car spinning out of control, it is completely concerned with chaos.

Entropy is a universal process that eventually makes everything a muddle. An agent of change and chaos, entropy collapses order into disorder, precludes predictability and removes distinction and individuation. Ever-present and unstoppable, entropy inexorably drags us towards the ultimate dissolution—the end of everything. And, since everything must end, it's what ties Ted Turner and television to the heat death of the universe. As the Gulf War coverage amply demonstrated, CNN and entropy both do exactly the same thing to understanding: they both make meaning incomprehensible.

"We live in the Age of Information," proclaims every bush-league Dr. Tomorrow with access to a platform, a PC, and a satellite dish, but no one seems to know what this actually means. Like McLuhan's "The Medium is the Message," the term has become a piece of verbal driftwood, so drenched in overuse that it no longer sparks inquiry, let alone under-standing. No one even seems to notice that it simply isn't true.

We don't live in the Age of Information; we live in the Age of Rumour.

We interrupt this program to tell you that... "Half the Iraqi air force has been destroyed on the ground" ... "Six chemical warheads have exploded in Tel Aviv" ... "An assassination attempt has been made on Saddam Hussein" ... "A milk plant has been destroyed" ... "Syria has invaded Iraq" ... "The war will be over by Christmas" ... We interrupt this program to lie to you.

Like a rumour, or a lie, entropy is missing information: information that affects understanding. Information in-forms; it literally shapes understanding. In its medieval—and mostly forgotten—sense, *information* meant something that gave a certain character or structure to both matter and mind.

Information theorists conceive of information in much the same way. They see information as a set of generative codes that bring order and structure to the entropic systems through the introduction of redundancy and predictability. Or, in more human-readable words, information brings order to the unexpected. It is the opposite of entropy. Information is the code which brings comprehension from chaos.

We inhabit a context of communicative chaos, always in danger of being inundated by billions of bits of information. Every second we receive roughly ten thousand bits of random data from our sense organs: an overwhelming onslaught which no one can completely process. Instead of trying to understand everything our senses send, we unconsciously use a set of communicative codes, informational criteria, which selects which data matters and which does not. And it is through this mixture of code and chaos, of information and entropy, that we make meaning.

Shortly after CNN stopped giving us the Gulf War from sunrise to sunrise, an unconfirmed report made its way into the academic press. The report stated that those who had spent the most time watching television coverage of the Gulf War actually understood it the least. Somehow, television took all the meaning out of Desert Storm; somehow, CNN just didn't make sense.

The Gulf War was the most reported conflict ever, a record only recently surpassed by its recent sequel. In fact, despite the heavy censorship imposed by the military on the mass media, there was more media information available on a daily basis on this single subject than on any other single story in television's history. Yet what television, and more specifically CNN, gave us wasn't news, it was noise.

▸

He arrived about an hour and a half late. There were about three hundred of us gathered in a small lecture hall at the University of Western Washington in Bellingham. We were there to see the founder and most famous practitioner of Gonzo journalism, Hunter S. Thompson, and we were getting pissed off.

Finally he arrived, accompanied by a bodyguard, a bottle

of Wild Turkey and a television set "liberated" from his hotel room. He flashed us an arms-upraised Nixon-style victory salute, announced that one of us would be the lucky winner of the TV set, and that he was all set for a "savage" political discussion.

"Let's go after the swine," he said, "especially Ed Meese. Not many people outside of Washington know this, but Meese was the star performer in the Vicki Morgan/Alfred Bloomingdale sex tapes."

Thompson went on in this vein for a while, and some apolitical pinhead yahoos, who only seemed to know Thompson from that bad movie with Bill Murray, began to get bored and angry, and stood up on the tables they had been squatting on and started chanting, "No politics, no politics! Dance, Duke, dance!" as the rest of the crowd tried to shout them down.

Seeing Thompson getting angry, and sensing things were falling apart, the organizers tried to restore order by opening the floor up to questions. And right away the unexpected happened, as this crazy guy ran up the aisle and grabbed the mic.

"What's it all about?" he yelled at Thompson. "What does it mean? I read, I watch TV, but I don't know . . . what does it all mean?"

Thompson looked at the guy for few seconds, asked if the place "was some sort of fucking business college" and then snarled, "How the fuck should I know? I'm just a working journalist. I don't have all the answers."

►

In its attempt to answer everything about every aspect of the entire Gulf War, regardless of whether the information was valid or even available, CNN turned the news into "noise."

Noise is information-theory jargon for anything that corrupts the integrity of a message. When communication is filled with noise, entropy is high, information is low, distinctions are lost, and meaning is diminished. Noise disrupts the order of understanding.

Somewhere in that grey triangle of confirmed, censored, and cleared, CNN tried to slot the news in the very second it happened. And those who watched the most understood the least. Somewhere in the never-ending flow of ever-changing updates, normal patterns of understanding collapsed, information was engulfed by entropy, and comprehension was consumed by confusion. News became noise in a deluge of data that didn't—and couldn't—distinguish fact from fiction.

It's fitting that no one ever gave an exact definition of the New World Order oft touted by Bush the Elder. Whatever it is—and I suspect it'll be a lot like high school with guns and money—the New World Order probably won't have a lot of meaning, as it emerges in concurrence with the information revolution. We may not all be Newtons, but we all possess a lot more facts than our brightest forebearers. We also know a lot fewer truths. CNN's senseless coverage of the first Gulf War is simply an early example what we all face in the current technological climate: a cacophony so loud and chaotic that we can't hear clearly above all the noise.

Welcome to the Age of Rumour.

Morrison became a movie about the same time the Gulf War ended. Both Bill Graham and Ray Manzarek, two close friends of Morrison's, denounced *The Doors* as a distortion of the truth. Many reviewers praised the movie's authenticity. A number of biographies and hundreds of articles were published around the same time. All of them claimed to give us some insight, some essential truth, about the life of the rock star. Meanwhile, somewhere beneath a graffiti-covered gravestone in Paris, the only person who knew the whole story, the star of the show, crumbled slowly into dust.

About the Author

JIM OATEN was the inaugural winner of *subTerrain*'s creative non-fiction award, and has had previous work published in *Vancouver Magazine, Vancouver Review, The Vancouver Sun, Pacific Rim* and *Where*. Mr. Oaten has recieved a National Magazine Award (Honourable Mention) and has been a Western Magazine Award finalist. Currently a denizen of East Vancouver, he lives in fear of real estate prices. *Accelerated Paces* is his first book.